A-LEVEL
STUDENT GUIDE

PEARSON EDEXCEL

Economics A

Theme 1

Introduction to markets and market failure

Mark Gavin

HODDER
EDUCATION
AN HACHETTE UK COMPANY

This Guide has been written specifically to support students preparing for the Pearson Edexcel A-level Economics A (Theme 1) examinations. The content has been neither approved nor endorsed by Edexcel and remains the sole responsibility of the author.

Every effort has been made to trace all copyright holders, but if any have been inadvertently overlooked, the Publishers will be pleased to make the necessary arrangements at the first opportunity.

Although every effort has been made to ensure that website addresses are correct at time of going to press, Hodder Education cannot be held responsible for the content of any website mentioned in this book. It is sometimes possible to find a relocated web page by typing in the address of the home page for a website in the URL window of your browser.

Hachette UK's policy is to use papers that are natural, renewable and recyclable products and made from wood grown in well-managed forests and other controlled sources. The logging and manufacturing processes are expected to conform to the environmental regulations of the country of origin.

Orders: please contact Bookpoint Ltd, 130 Park Drive, Milton Park, Abingdon, Oxon OX14 4SE. Telephone: (44) 01235 827827. Fax: (44) 01235 400401. Email: education@bookpoint.co.uk. Lines are open from 9 a.m. to 5 p.m., Monday to Saturday, with a 24-hour message answering service. You can also order through our website: www.hoddereducation.co.uk.

© Mark Gavin 2019

ISBN 978-1-5104-5804-8

First printed 2019

First published in 2019 by
Hodder Education,
An Hachette UK Company
Carmelite House
50 Victoria Embankment
London EC4Y 0DZ

www.hoddereducation.co.uk

Impression number 10 9 8 7 6 5 4 3 2 1

Year   2023 2022 2021 2020 2019

Cover photo: Tomasz Zajda/Adobe Stock

Typeset by Integra Software Services Pvt. Ltd, Pondicherry, India

Printed in Italy

A catalogue record for this title is available from the British Library.

MIX
Paper from
responsible sources
FSC™ C104740

Contents

Content Guidance

Questions & Answers

■ Getting the most from this book

Exam tips

Advice on key points in the text to help you learn and recall content, avoid pitfalls, and polish your exam technique in order to boost your grade.

Knowledge check

Rapid-fire questions throughout the Content Guidance section to check your understanding.

Knowledge check answers

1 Turn to the back of the book for the Knowledge check answers.

Summaries

■ Each core topic is rounded off by a bullet-list summary for quick-check reference of what you need to know.

Exam-style questions

Commentary on the questions

Tips on what you need to do to gain full marks.

Sample student answers

Practise the questions, then look at the student answers that follow.

Commentary on sample student answers

Read the comments showing how many marks each answer would be awarded in the exam and exactly where marks are gained or lost.

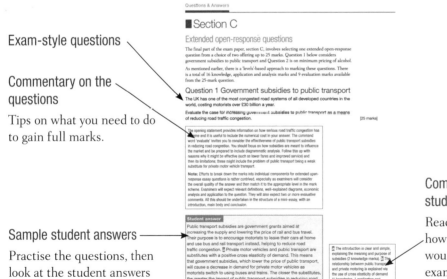

■About this book

The Pearson Edexcel A-level Economics A specification is structured into four themes and consists of three exam papers. The aim of this guide is to help you prepare for Paper 1 (code 9EC0/01). Paper 1 'Markets and business behaviour' tests models and concepts from Themes 1 and 3. Consequently, it is important to study both themes ('Introduction to markets and market failure' and 'Business behaviour and the labour market') in preparation for taking exam Paper 1.

This guide includes all the topics for Theme 1 and comprises around half the content required for Paper 1. The concepts and models covered in this guide also feed directly into the synoptic A-level Paper 3, 'Microeconomics and macroeconomics' (code 9EC0/03).

This guide should be used as a supplement to a taught course along with textbooks and other materials recommended by your teacher. There are two sections:

■ The **Content Guidance** section summarises the specification content of Theme 1. Theme 1 is based on the price mechanism model, which underpins the whole specification. Theme 1's content comprises four main topics. A summary of key points is provided at the end of each topic in this guide.
■ The **Questions & Answers** section provides guidance on how to answer the A-level exam Paper 1, particularly the topics covering markets and market failure. It includes multiple-choice and short-answer questions, data-response questions and extended open-response questions. It also includes student answers and comments on how to improve performance.

Exam format

Paper 1, 'Markets and business behaviour', has three sections.

Section A comprises five compulsory questions worth a total of 25 marks. Each of these five questions comprises a multiple-choice question (worth 1 mark) and either one short-answer question or two short-answer questions.

Section B comprises one compulsory data-response question broken down into five parts and worth a total of 50 marks. The mark allocations for these parts are as follows: 5, 8, 10, 12 and 15.

Section C is an extended open-response question (mini-essay) where students select one from a choice of two options. This is worth 25 marks.

The time allowed for the examination is 2 hours.

Note that Paper 1 requires students to answer questions from Theme 1, 'Introduction to markets and market failure', and Theme 3, 'Business behaviour and the labour market'. Students are required to learn the models and concepts from both themes in preparation for the exam. You are therefore advised to obtain the accompanying student guide in this series, 'Business behaviour and the labour market', which provides further guidance on the content and exam questions for Theme 3.

Content Guidance

■ The nature of economics

Economics as a social science

Economics is a social science, which means it is concerned with the study of human behaviour. It investigates how scarce resources are allocated to provide for unlimited human wants. Economists develop models which attempt to simplify and improve our understanding of how consumers and producers behave. These models include assumptions: for example, consumers aim to maximise satisfaction or utility when spending their income. Similarly, producers aim to maximise profits from the goods and services they make and sell. Economic models are judged upon their ability to explain and predict consumer and producer behaviour, even when the assumptions of such models are unrealistic.

Economics The allocation of scarce resources to provide for unlimited human wants.

Thinking like an economist requires use of the **ceteris paribus** assumption. It means 'all other things being equal' or 'all other things remaining the same'. This assumption is needed since economists cannot test models in scientifically controlled laboratory conditions. For example, a bakery may cut the price of chocolate cakes and find that more are demanded or purchased. This leads to the construction of a demand curve depicting an inverse relationship between the price and quantity purchased of chocolate cakes. However, we have to assume that other things remain the same: for example, the level of consumer income, advertising and the price of other types of cakes. Otherwise, a change in any one of these factors could be the cause of more chocolate cakes being demanded.

Ceteris paribus 'All other things being equal'.

Positive and normative economic statements

Positive economics

Positive economics is concerned with facts and is value-free. It is a scientific approach to the discipline, where economists explain the outcome of a particular policy, but are not expected to take sides. Positive statements can be tested as true or false by referring to the facts.

An example of a **positive statement** is: 'The increase in the National Living Wage from £7.83 to £8.21 per hour in April 2019 has caused unemployment.' It is possible to check the facts by appealing to authoritative sources and see whether this has increased unemployment or not. The statement can be accepted as true or rejected as false.

Positive economics statement Based on facts which can be tested as true or false and are value-free.

Normative economics

Normative economics is concerned with value judgements and is a non-scientific approach to the discipline. A normative statement is an expression that something is right or wrong, so it often includes the words ought, should, fair, unfair, better or worse.

An example of a **normative statement** is: 'It is unfair to cut welfare benefits to poor people.' The term 'unfair' is a value judgement which one can agree or disagree with. It is not possible to prove or disprove it, but rather, it depends upon the values held by individuals.

Role of value judgements in economic decision making and policy

Value judgements have a major influence on economic decision making for consumers and producers. Personal preferences, beliefs and subjective assessment underpin normative economics. For example, a highly cautious individual may prefer to save more of his or her income in a pension fund rather than increase current spending on consumer goods; similarly, a producer prone to taking high risks may prefer to spend cash reserves on developing new goods rather than have a safety net for unanticipated future events.

Value judgements also have a major role in government policy making. For example, a government may prefer to cut income tax rather than increase expenditure on healthcare provision. This could be due to an underlying preference for the operation of free market forces rather than more government intervention in an economy.

The economic problem

The economic problem is based on **scarcity**. Scarcity arises because there are insufficient resources to provide for everyone's wants. It occurs in all economies, since resources are finite compared to human material wants. Scarcity is obvious in countries that face famine or drought, where insufficient food or water is available to meet everyone's needs. However, scarcity also exists in wealthy countries, since not all human material wants can be satisfied.

Scarcity means we have to make choices over the use of our limited resources to provide for our material wants. Some crucial decisions have to be made over what, how and for whom to produce. These decisions are faced by consumers, producers and the government. Once a decision has been made about what to use a resource for, opportunity cost arises.

Opportunity costs to economic agents

Opportunity cost refers to the value of the next best alternative forgone. Consumers, producers and governments all face opportunity cost.

A consumer may have £25 available to spend on a meal at a restaurant or on the next best thing, which is a new T-shirt. The individual cannot buy both at the same time. If the consumer chooses to buy a meal then the opportunity cost is forgoing the new T-shirt.

Exam tip

Use the term 'value judgement' rather than 'opinion' when explaining a normative economic statement.

Normative economics statement Based on value judgements which cannot be tested as true or false.

Exam tip

Always use the information provided to explain why a statement Is normative: tor example, normative statements are often characterised by value-laden words such as fair, unfair, better, worse, should and ought.

Scarcity There are finite resources compared to infinite human wants, so choices have to be made about how to use those resources.

Opportunity cost The value of the next best alternative forgone.

A firm may have £50,000 available to invest in a new machine or to invest in a training programme for employees. The managers have to make a choice over the best use of the funds.

A government may have an extra £100 million of tax revenue. It might use this to build a new hospital but, in doing so, forgoes the building of a large school, considered to be the next best alternative.

Opportunity cost often involves the use of **marginal analysis** — to gain one extra unit of a good means that resources have been transferred from the production of another good.

Renewable and non-renewable resources

Resources, or factors of production, are inputs used in the production of goods and services. They are finite and can be classified into four types: land, labour, capital and enterprise.

A **renewable resource** is one whose stock level can be replenished naturally over a period of time. Such resources include solar energy, wind power, tidal power, fish, timber and soil. However, renewable resources may decline over time if they are consumed at a faster rate than the environment can replenish them. They require careful management, to avoid such things as deforestation and soil erosion.

A **non-renewable resource** is one whose stock level decreases over time as it is consumed. These resources include fossil fuels such as coal, oil and gas. They also include commodities such as steel, copper and aluminium. It is possible to reduce the rate of decline of non-renewable resources through recycling, the development of substitutes and new technology. The price mechanism also has a role to play in reducing the rate of consumption via higher prices.

Production possibility frontiers

A production possibility frontier shows the maximum potential level of output for two goods or services that an economy can achieve when all its resources are fully and efficiently employed, given the level of technology available. It can be used to illustrate scarcity and opportunity cost.

Movement along a production possibility frontier

Figure 1 shows the production possibility frontier of an economy with capital and consumer goods. **Consumer goods** directly provide satisfaction or utility to consumers. They are wanted for their own sake rather than for what they produce. Examples include clothing, food, drink, a holiday and iPhones. **Capital goods** are used to produce more consumer goods and services. Generally, they provide satisfaction to consumers indirectly. Examples include machinery, office blocks, training of workers and factories.

Marginal analysis
The effects of producing or consuming one extra unit of a good or service — they may involve both benefits and costs.

Knowledge check 1

What is the opportunity cost of you staying on at school or college to study A-levels?

Renewable resource
A resource whose stock level can be replenished naturally over a period of time.

Non-renewable resource A resource whose stock level decreases over time as it is consumed.

Consumer good A good, such as a chocolate bar, that directly provides utility to consumers. It is wanted for the satisfaction it gives.

Capital good A good that is used to produce consumer goods or services, such as a machine that helps make chocolate bars. It is wanted not for its own sake, but rather for the consumer goods and services it can produce.

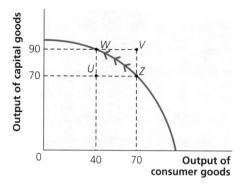

Figure 1 Production possibility frontier

Initially, the economy is at point Z. To increase the production of capital goods by 20 units and move to point W, there is an opportunity cost of 30 units of consumer goods.

The movement from Z to W increases the rate of economic growth, since capital goods are crucial for increasing production. Economic growth can be shown by an outward shift of the production possibility frontier. However, the loss of 30 units of consumer goods means that current living standards will fall in order to enable future living standards to rise at a faster rate.

If the economy is located at any point on its **production possibility frontier**, there is an efficient allocation of resources, since none are being wasted. However, if the economy is located within its production possibility frontier, there is an inefficient allocation of resources as not all are being used. At position U it is possible to increase production of both consumer and capital goods, by utilising unemployed resources. Since nothing is given up in return, there is no opportunity cost.

Position V shows an output combination that is currently unobtainable, given the availability of resources and level of technology. The production possibility frontier will need to shift outwards in order to reach this combination of output of capital and consumer goods.

The shape of production possibility frontiers: curves and straight lines

A typical production possibility frontier is bowed to the origin and shows that, as more of one good is produced, an increasing amount of the other good is forgone. The opportunity cost rises. This is because not all resources are as efficient as other resources in the production of both goods. Diminishing returns set in.

A good example is the use of agricultural land in East Anglia and southwest England. We can assume that farmland can be used either for growing wheat or for livestock production. East Anglia has highly fertile and light soils with suitable rainfall for growing wheat. Output per acre is very high. However, as we move towards the southwest, the soil becomes too heavy and rainfall too high for growing wheat. Instead, livestock farming is far more productive per acre. If farmland in the southwest were converted to wheat production, yields would be very low and would be achieved only at a cost of forgoing considerable livestock output.

Production possibility frontier The maximum potential output of a combination of goods an economy can achieve when all its resources are fully and efficiently employed, given the current level of technology.

Knowledge check 2

How might opportunity cost be shown on a production possibility frontier?

Exam tip

Be prepared to define key economic concepts in data-response and in open-response questions as knowledge marks are often awarded for this.

Shifts in the production possibility frontier

A country's production potential may increase over time, which is shown in Figure 2 by an outward shift in its production possibility frontier. This represents economic growth and there are a number of possible causes: for example, an increase in the quantity or quality of resources; the expansion of further and higher education and government training schemes; or an increase in investment and the development of new technology.

Exam tip

Be prepared to annotate or draw a diagram of a production possibility frontier when answering short-answer and data-response questions on this concept. Marks are usually available for this.

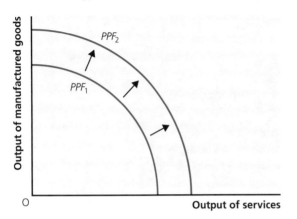

Figure 2 An increase in the production possibility frontier

Occasionally the production possibility frontier may shift inwards towards the origin, indicating a decrease in the potential output of an economy. This may be caused by war or a natural disaster where many resources are destroyed. In 2017 Hurricane Irma devastated parts of Texas and Florida in the United States, causing up to $200 billion of damage and reducing productive capacity.

Knowledge check 3

What is the state of the economy if it is operating at a point within its production possibility frontier?

Knowledge check 4

Outline the factors which might lead to an outward shift of the production possibility frontier for a country.

Specialisation and the division of labour

Specialisation occurs when an individual, a firm, a region or a country concentrates on the production of a limited range of goods and services. The advantages of specialisation are that it increases productivity and living standards across the world. The UK specialises in the production of medicinal drugs, aircraft manufacture, tourism, and financial and business services. These goods and services can then be traded for other goods and services produced by other countries. It leads to a higher level of global output and higher living standards.

Specialisation can have disadvantages, notably when demand for a good or service falls, leading to a significant increase in structural unemployment. Also, a country specialising in the production and export of minerals may face problems of resource depletion. Another problem relates to the price at which goods are sold: for example, many developing countries face an unfavourable rate of exchange, selling their commodities at a low price compared to the goods they purchase from overseas.

The **division of labour** is one form of specialisation, where individuals concentrate on the production of a particular good or service. Production is broken down into a series of tasks, conducted by different workers. For example, house construction involves a range of specialist labour, including architects, surveyors, bricklayers,

Specialisation When an individual, firm, region or country concentrates on the production of a limited range of goods and services.

Division of labour The specialisation of workers on individual tasks in the production process to increase efficiency.

carpenters and electricians. Adam Smith, the first ever professor of economics, writing in the eighteenth century, explained division of labour by referring to production in a pin factory. He explained that by breaking down pin production into 18 specialist tasks, each carried out by a different worker, total output of pins increased by 2,000%, compared to a situation where each worker had to carry out all the tasks involved.

Advantages of the division of labour

- Increase in labour productivity (higher output per worker per hour), which leads to higher living standards. Each worker can become highly skilled in a task due to repetition: for example, a tyre fitter in a garage.
- Increase in the efficiency of resources, helping to reduce the cost per unit of output. This is partly because capital equipment can be used continuously on a production line: for example, robots on motor vehicle assembly lines. In addition, no time is wasted in moving workers from one task to another: for example, packers on a sandwich production line. Furthermore, less time is required to train workers for specific tasks: for example, training a chef to make pastry dishes rather than training him or her in all aspects of cooking food in a restaurant.
- Increase in the quality of output since each worker can specialise in a job that suits his or her skills, aptitude and experience. For example, a person who likes rock climbing might specialise in work as an outdoor pursuits leader and become highly proficient.

Disadvantages of the division of labour

- Repetition creates monotony and boredom. There could be a high turnover of staff, leading to increased recruitment and selection costs.
- Breaking down production into different tasks makes it easier to replace skilled workers with machines, leading to structural unemployment, such as motor vehicle paint sprayers being replaced by robots, or supermarket cashiers being replaced with self-service scanning machines.
- Specialisation creates interdependence in production. If one group of workers goes on strike, it could halt production across the whole industry. For example, when train drivers call a one-day stoppage, they disrupt the work of guards and ticket inspectors, as well as that of many commuters.

The functions of money

Money is anything that is generally acceptable in the payment of a good or service, or of a debt. Money comes in various forms, largely in cash and bank deposits. Advances in technology mean we are moving towards a cashless society where most payments occur through debiting and crediting bank accounts. The development of money enabled specialisation and trade to grow, leading to the sophisticated economies of today. It is crucial that people have confidence in the money used; otherwise it will lose its general acceptability for making transactions. Once this happens, it ceases to be money. An example of this problem is in Venezuela where the government printed off too much of its currency (the bolivar), leading to hyperinflation. In 2019 the inflation rate exceeded 2 million per cent, with the currency becoming worthless and so no longer acceptable in payment for goods and services.

Exam tip

Be careful not to confuse an increase in total production costs with a decrease in cost per unit of output. Specialisation will typically increase total production costs for a firm, since it is likely to increase total output, requiring more raw materials and machinery. However, it also leads to a reduction in the cost per unit of output, since workers become more productive.

Knowledge check 5

Why does the division of labour increase productivity or output per head?

Money Anything that is generally acceptable in the payment of a good or service, or of a debt.

There are four functions of money:

- *Medium of exchange*. It enables the buying and selling of products, making exchange easier. Money eliminates the need for barter.
- *Measure of value*. It enables a value to be placed on products so they can be bought and sold with ease. Money creates a unit of measure that enables comparisons between the relative values of products.
- *Store of value*. It is a convenient way of storing wealth so that it can be spent at a later date. Money will tend to hold its value in the short term as long as inflation remains low.
- *Method of deferred payment*. It enables borrowing and lending. This means someone can borrow money in order to buy a product rather than waiting until enough funds have been saved. A price is usually set for borrowing and lending — this is known as the rate of interest.

Free market, mixed and command economies

An economy organises its resources in different ways to produce goods and services. This ranges along a continuum from a free market economy through to a mixed economy and then a command economy. Figure 3 shows the notion of a continuum.

Percentage of resources allocated by the price mechanism

100%	50%	0%
Free market economy	**Mixed economy**	**Command economy**
All resources are allocated by the price mechanism. No government intervention.	Some resources are allocated by the price mechanism and some by the government.	All resources are allocated by the government. No price mechanism.

Figure 3 Types of economic system

In reality, the vast majority of economies comprise a mixture of both private enterprise (the private sector) and state intervention (the public sector), thus being mixed economies. In the UK around 60% of resources are allocated by the private sector and 40% by the public sector. The government is a major provider of education, healthcare, defence and law and order in society. In other European economies (e.g. France, Germany and Sweden), the size of the public sector is greater, while in North America (the USA and Canada) it is lower. In all cases these are considered to be mixed economies.

A free market economy

A **free market economy** is where decisions on what, how and for whom to produce are left to the operation of the price mechanism. It is associated with the writings of the economists Adam Smith and Friedrich Hayek. In a free market economy, resources are privately owned and economic decision making is decentralised among many individual consumers and producers. There is minimum government intervention.

Free market economy
Where all resources are privately owned and allocated via the price mechanism. There is minimal government intervention.

In his famous book *The Wealth of Nations*, published in 1776, Smith referred to the 'invisible hand' of self-interest as guiding supply and demand in markets. He believed that consumers and producers acting in their own self-interest would lead to the best outcome for all in society. This approach led to the development of the classical school of economic thought.

There are no pure free market economies in the world today since, in every economy, the government directly controls some resources and output. However, the proportion of government intervention tends to be significantly less in some developing countries, such as Malaysia and Thailand, compared to the developed world. Perhaps the best example of a developed country with a relatively small government sector is Hong Kong.

Advantages of a free market economy

- Economic efficiency and lower prices: competition means that firms try to keep production costs down in order to sell goods and services at competitive prices (productive efficiency). Competition also means that firms try to produce goods and services that consumers demand (allocative efficiency). This means the price mechanism will equate consumer demand with producer supply.
- Quality of products: competition means firms continuously try to improve the quality of their products to gain an advantage over rivals. There is considerable consumer sovereignty: that is, consumer power in the market.
- Greater choice: consumers can often choose to buy from a wide selection of goods and services; workers often have a wide choice of employment opportunities.
- Financial incentives: entrepreneurs have an incentive to invest and take risks in order to earn profit; labour has an incentive to work hard to gain more earnings.

Disadvantages of a free market economy

- Monopolies may form as a result of competition in some markets; rival firms get taken over or go out of business.
- The distribution of income and wealth is very unequal and the lack of welfare support may lead to people living in absolute poverty.
- External costs and benefits from production or consumption are sometimes ignored. For example, the price mechanism ignores the external costs of pollution and the external benefits of education.
- Information gaps persist: people may consume excessive amounts of demerit goods such as drugs, tobacco and alcohol, unaware of their dangers. There is a lack of regulations and taxation to protect consumers.
- An insufficient quantity of public goods and merit goods is provided in a market economy. Public goods include defence and street lighting, while merit goods include healthcare and education.
- Erratic swings in the business cycle may cause high inflation during an economic boom and high unemployment during an economic slump.

A command economy

This is an economy where the government makes the decisions on what, how and for whom to produce. It is associated with the writings of Karl Marx, a nineteenth-century economist and philosopher who believed that production should be directed on the basis of human need rather than profit. In a **command economy**, the government has control of resources and economic decision making is centralised. There is no role for the price mechanism. Command economies can work effectively during times of national crisis: for example, the UK was run like one during the Second World War with great success. However, personal freedom and living standards tend to be jeopardised in such economic systems. One example today is North Korea.

Command economy
Where there is public ownership of resources and these are allocated by the government.

Advantages of a command economy

- Cooperation between firms can lead to high levels of output. In general, the maximisation of output replaces the maximisation of profits as the key aim of firms.
- There is a reduction in inequality compared to free market economies, since the government controls the wages of all workers.
- The government may limit the external costs from production and consumption: for example, it can limit pollution emissions from firms and place severe taxes on harmful products such as tobacco and alcohol.
- The government can fund the provision of public goods such as defence and law and order; it can also increase the provision of goods which yield high external benefits to society, such as education and healthcare.
- The government has more control of the economy and so there are smaller swings in the business cycle, leading to less unemployment and inflation.

Disadvantages of a command economy

- The price mechanism is unable to operate and so markets may suffer from shortages (excess demand) and surpluses (excess supply), leading to an inefficient allocation of resources.
- The lack of competition between firms leads to inefficiency, and so productivity is low.
- The lack of competition leads to poor-quality products, especially when the emphasis is on maximising output rather than profit.
- There is less choice of goods and services for consumers to select from; labour may also be directed into specific jobs with no choice depending on their location.
- A lack of financial incentives: managers have no profit incentive to take risks by developing new goods and services, as the focus is on maximising output; labour has little incentive to work hard, since wages are fixed by the government.
- Under-performance of command economies: economic growth and living standards tend to grow at a much slower rate than in market-based economies. This was a major cause of the collapse of the Soviet Union during the early 1990s.

Exam tip

Note that the advantages of a command economy tend to represent disadvantages of a free market economy; similarly, the disadvantages of a command economy often represent advantages of a free market economy.

A mixed economy

This is an economy where decisions on what, how and for whom to produce are made partly by the private sector and partly by the government. Most developed countries in the world today fall under this classification. Examples are the UK, USA, France, Germany, Canada, Australia and Sweden.

The rationale of a **mixed economy** is to gain the advantages of the market economy while avoiding its disadvantages through government intervention. It is associated with the writings of John Maynard Keynes in the early twentieth century. Often

Mixed economy Where some resources are owned and allocated by the private sector and some by the public sector.

government intervention occurs to correct market failure: for example, the under-provision of merit goods such as education and healthcare or the non-provision of public goods such as defence. Government intervention usually arises to help markets work more effectively.

Summary

- Economics is concerned with how resources are allocated to provide for human wants. As resources are finite, there is an opportunity cost in producing a good or service, since the resources could have been used to produce alternative goods or services.
- Positive economic statements are facts which can be tested as true or false, whereas normative economic statements are value judgements which cannot be tested as true or false.
- The production possibility frontier illustrates the concepts of finite resources and opportunity cost. It can also be used to show unemployment and economic growth.
- Specialisation and the division of labour have led to huge increases in productivity.
- Money is anything that is generally acceptable in the payment of goods and services, or of debts. It has four functions: a medium of exchange, a measure of value, a store of value and a method of deferred payment.
- Most economies are mixed economies, where resources are allocated partly by private enterprise and partly by the government.

Knowledge check 6

Which type of economic system best describes the UK?

■ How markets work

Rational decision making in the market

There are many types of **market**: for example, clothing, motor vehicles and housing markets. One thing they have in common is that buyers and sellers come into contact for the purpose of exchange. A price is agreed for exchange to take place. By price, we mean the exchange value of a good or service. Buyers or consumers represent the 'demand' side of the market and sellers or producers represent the 'supply' side of the market.

Consumers are assumed to make rational decisions. This means consumers will allocate their income to maximise their utility or satisfaction from the goods and services they purchase. **Utility** refers to the amount of satisfaction obtained from consuming a good or service. Economists often make the assumption that utility can be measured.

Producers are also assumed to make **rational decisions**. This means firms will use their resources to maximise profits from the goods and services produced. This involves producing at the level of output where total revenue exceeds total cost by the largest amount.

Rational decision making is based on consumers and producers having:

- perfect market information
- computational skills and judgemental skills
- the ability to take decisions free from the behaviour of others
- sufficient time to take decisions

In reality, both consumers and producers often lack market knowledge as well as the skills and time to make rational decisions, free from the influence and the behaviour of others. Consequently, they may not always make decisions that maximise utility and profits.

Demand

The buyers or consumers in a market are said to demand goods or services. **Demand** refers to the quantity of a good or service purchased at a given price over a given time period. Demand is different from just wanting a good or service. It is a want backed up by the ability to pay, which is also known as effective demand.

Movement along a demand curve

A **demand curve** shows the quantity of a good or service that would be bought over a range of different price levels in a given period of time. The demand curve for a good slopes downwards from left to right because, as price falls, the good becomes cheaper compared to substitute goods and also more can be purchased with a given level of income.

The market demand curve is the horizontal summation of each individual demand curve for a particular good or service.

Market Where consumers and producers come into contact with each other to exchange goods and services.

Utility The amount of satisfaction obtained from consuming a good or service.

Rational decision making Where consumers allocate their expenditure on goods and services to maximise utility, and producers allocate their resources to maximise profits.

Demand The quantity of a good or service purchased at a given price over a given time period.

Demand curve Shows the quantity of a good or service that would be bought over a range of different price levels in a given period of time.

There is a movement along a demand curve for a good only when there is a change in its price. A fall in price causes an extension in demand, and a rise in price causes a contraction in demand, as shown in Figure 4.

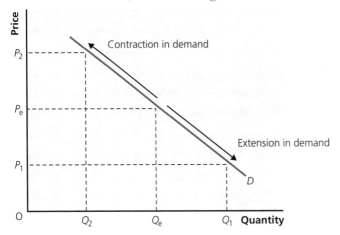

Figure 4 Movement along a demand curve

Marginal utility and the downward-sloping demand curve

The downward-sloping demand curve can also be explained by the concept of diminishing **marginal utility**. As one consumes more of a good, the utility or satisfaction gained from each extra unit will tend to fall or diminish. For example, at breakfast, the first bowl of cornflakes might give a high level of utility if one is hungry. However, a second bowl will not provide as much utility as the first, since one is less hungry. A third bowl of cornflakes will provide even less utility than the second bowl as one becomes full. This is an example of the law of **diminishing marginal utility**.

Note that total utility from consuming the bowls of cornflakes will increase as more is consumed, but this occurs at a diminishing rate. Eventually, one might feel sick from eating too many cornflakes and so marginal utility could fall drastically.

As marginal utility falls from each extra good consumed, it means consumers will only buy more of it if the price falls — hence the downward-sloping demand curve. Figure 5 shows the relationship between marginal utility, total utility and the amount of a good consumed.

Marginal utility The utility or satisfaction obtained from consuming one extra unit of a good or service.

Diminishing marginal utility As successive units of a good are consumed, the utility gained from each extra unit will fall.

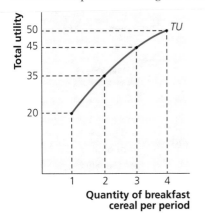 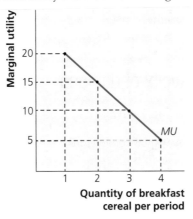

Figure 5 Total utility, marginal utility and the amount of a good consumed

Knowledge check 7

Why does the demand curve slope downwards from left to right?

Knowledge check 8

What causes a movement along a demand curve for a good?

Shifts in the demand curve

An increase in demand refers to the whole demand curve shifting outwards to the right at every price level. A decrease in demand refers to the whole demand curve shifting inwards to the left at every price level.

There are various factors which can shift the demand curve for a good. For example, the demand for Sony PlayStation 4 games consoles might increase due to:

- a fall in the price of complementary goods, such as computer games (Grand Theft Auto and FIFA Soccer)
- a rise in the price of substitute goods, such as the Microsoft Xbox One or the Nintendo Wii games consoles
- a change in fashion and tastes which makes games consoles more popular as a leisure activity among young people
- increased advertising of PlayStation games and consoles
- an increase in real incomes (for normal goods), meaning that the PlayStation becomes more affordable for people to buy
- a decrease in income tax, which leads to an increase in disposable income so that a PlayStation console becomes more affordable
- an increase in the population or a change in the age structure of the population so that there are more teenagers likely to purchase a PlayStation games console
- an increase in credit facilities, which makes it easier to obtain funds to pay for a PlayStation games console

Figure 6 shows a decrease in demand by the shift of the demand curve leftwards to D_1 and an increase in demand is demonstrated by a rightward shift to D_2.

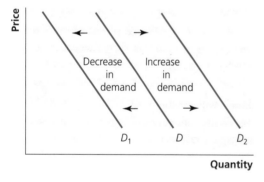

Figure 6 Shifts in demand curves

Price, income and cross elasticity of demand

Price elasticity of demand

Price elasticity of demand (*PED*) is the responsiveness of the demand for a good to a change in its price. The formula to calculate it is:

$$PED = \frac{\text{percentage change in quantity demanded of good A}}{\text{percentage change in price of good A}}$$

Price elasticity of demand The responsiveness of demand for a good or service to a change in its price.

In most circumstances, a minus answer is obtained, indicating that the two variables of price and demand move in opposite directions. There is a negative gradient.

Types of price elasticity of demand

If *PED* is greater than 1, the good is relatively price elastic: that is, the percentage change in demand is greater than the percentage change in price. For example, a 10% rise in the price of holidays to Florida may cause a 20% decrease in the quantity demanded; *PED* is −2.

If *PED* is less than 1, the good is relatively price inelastic: that is, the percentage change in demand is less than the percentage change in price. For example, a 10% fall in price of coffee may cause a 5% increase in the quantity demanded; *PED* is −0.5.

If *PED* is equal to 1, the good has unit elasticity: that is, the percentage change in demand is the same as the percentage change in price. For example, a 10% fall in the price of apples may cause a 10% rise in the quantity demanded; *PED* is −1.

If *PED* is equal to zero, the good is perfectly inelastic: that is, a change in price has no effect on the quantity demanded. The demand curve is vertical. An example might be heroin to a drug addict.

If *PED* is infinite, the good is perfectly elastic: that is, a rise in price causes demand to fall to zero. The demand curve is horizontal.

The demand curves in Figure 7 show the different elasticities.

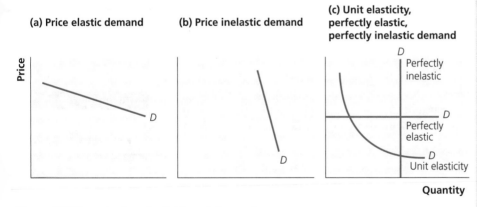

Figure 7 Different price elasticities of demand

The relationship between price elasticity of demand and total revenue

Elasticity varies along a straight-line demand curve, as shown in Figure 8. Elasticity falls as you move along the curve from the top left to the bottom right. At the mid-point, demand has unit elasticity.

Knowledge check 10

What does the minus sign mean in price elasticity of demand answers?

Knowledge check 11

What does the actual figure represent in price elasticity of demand answers?

Exam tip

Do not confuse elasticity with the gradient of a demand curve. Straight-line demand curves have constant gradients but different elasticities along them.

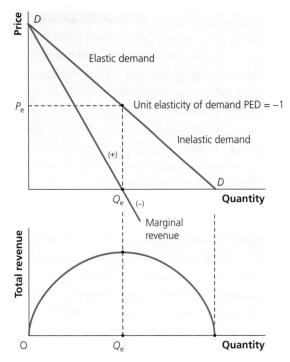

Figure 8 The relationship between price elasticity of demand and total revenue

Total revenue

Total revenue refers to the total payments a firm receives from selling a given quantity of goods or services. It is the price per unit of a good multiplied by the quantity sold. The total revenue a firm receives from selling a good will be equal to the total spending by consumers on that good.

A firm's total revenue will increase as long as price is moving towards the mid-position of the demand curve (where there is unit elasticity). It is important for firms to know the *PED* of their output when making pricing decisions, because this affects revenue and profitability.

If demand is elastic, then a cut in price increases total consumer spending and hence revenue to the firm. On the other hand, a rise in price causes total consumer spending to fall and so firms lose revenue.

If demand is inelastic, then an increase in price increases total consumer spending and hence revenue to the firm. On the other hand, a fall in price causes total consumer spending to fall and so firms lose revenue.

Once unit price elasticity has been reached, the firm is maximising its total revenue. Note the relationship between *PED* and **marginal revenue**, which falls during a move down the demand curve. As long as marginal revenue is positive, demand is price elastic. When marginal revenue is zero, demand is unit elastic; when marginal revenue is negative, demand is inelastic.

Total revenue The price per unit of a good multiplied by the quantity sold.

Knowledge check 12

Why might price elasticity of demand be useful to firms?

Marginal revenue Revenue gained by a firm from selling one extra unit of output.

Knowledge check 13

Why might price elasticity of demand be useful to the government?

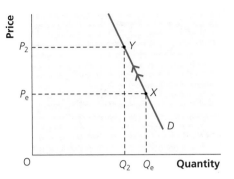

Figure 9 A rise in price increases total revenue under inelastic demand

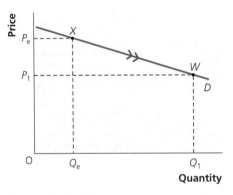

Figure 10 A fall in price increases total revenue under elastic demand

> **Exam tip**
>
> Be prepared to draw a diagram to show how a change in price will affect total revenue. For example, a rise in price will increase total revenue from OP_eXQ_e to OP_2YQ_2 when demand is inelastic (Figure 9); a fall in price will increase total revenue from OP_eXQ_e to OP_1WQ_1 when demand is elastic (Figure 10).

Determinants of price elasticity of demand

- *Availability of substitutes.* The more narrowly a good is defined, the more substitutes it tends to have and so its demand is price elastic. For example, cod, a type of fish, has many substitutes such as plaice, rock, salmon and haddock. However, the more broadly a good is defined, the fewer substitutes it tends to have and so its demand is less price elastic. For example, there are few close substitutes for fish as a whole and so demand tends to be relatively less elastic.
- *Luxury and necessity goods.* Luxury goods, such as racing cars and caviar, tend to have a price elastic demand, whereas necessity goods, like bread and underwear, tend to have a price inelastic demand.
- *Proportion of income spent on the good.* If a high percentage of income is spent on the good, as with a new car or boat, demand tends to be price elastic. However, for goods that take up a small percentage of income, such as newspapers and tomato sauce, demand will tend to be price inelastic.
- *Addictive and habit-forming goods.* Tobacco, alcohol and coffee are types of goods that tend to be price inelastic in demand.
- *The time period.* For most goods, demand is less elastic in the short run than in the long run. For example, a rise in the price of household electricity is likely to have only a minor effect on consumption in the short run. In the long run, households can cut back on consumption by switching to gas for their cooking and heating. This means demand eventually becomes more responsive to changes in price.

■ *Brand image.* Some goods have a strong brand image: for example, Levi jeans and Coca Cola. Demand for these goods is typically price inelastic as consumers are often willing to pay a premium price for them.

Income elasticity of demand

Income elasticity of demand (*YED*) is the responsiveness of demand for a good or service to a change in real income. (Real income refers to the spending power of money income — the amount of goods and services which can be purchased with one's nominal income.) The formula to calculate *YED* is:

$$YED = \frac{\text{percentage change in demand for a good}}{\text{percentage change in real income}}$$

> **Income elasticity of demand** The responsiveness of demand for a good or service to a change in real income.

> **Exam tip**
>
> Always show your workings in elasticity calculations and be careful to place the decimal point correctly. Marks are usually awarded for the workings even if the final answer is incorrect.

Normal goods

In most circumstances *YED* is positive, which means the two variables of income and demand move in the same direction. In other words, a rise in income causes a rise in quantity demanded. Note that some economists identify goods which have a *YED* above +1 as luxury goods. These are still a type of **normal good**.

A good with a *YED* less than 1 is relatively income inelastic and one with a *YED* above 1 is relatively income elastic in demand. The latter is often referred to as a luxury good. A *YED* of 1 means it has unitary elasticity.

> **Normal good** A good with a positive income elasticity of demand. As real income rises, so too does demand for the good.

Inferior goods

Occasionally, *YED* is negative which means the two variables of income and demand move in opposite directions. This is because people tend to demand higher-quality goods as their incomes rise, substituting them for lower-quality products. Figure 11 shows the demand curve for an **inferior good** compared with that of a normal good in relation to income. Examples of inferior goods are minced meat and supermarkets' own value brands of food.

> **Inferior good** A good with a negative income elasticity of demand. As real income rises, demand for the good falls.

> **Exam tip**
>
> If there is a fall in demand or a fall in income, always show the minus signs in your calculations. It will increase your chances of gaining full marks.

(a) Normal good

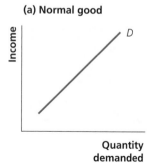

(b) Inferior good

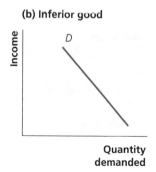

Figure 11 Income elasticity of demand

> **Knowledge check 14**
>
> Distinguish between normal and inferior goods.

Cross elasticity of demand

Cross elasticity of demand (*XED*) is the responsiveness of demand for good B to a change in price of good A. The formula to calculate *XED* is:

$$XED = \frac{\text{percentage change in demand for good B}}{\text{percentage change in price of good A}}$$

Cross elasticity of demand The responsiveness of demand for good B to a change in price of good A.

> **Exam tip**
>
> A common mistake students make with cross elasticity of demand is to refer to the change in demand for one good affecting the change in demand for another good. This would lead to selection of the incorrect option in multiple-choice questions. Instead, it refers to how a change in price of one good affects the demand for another good.

Cross elasticity of demand is used to determine whether goods are complements or substitutes for each other.

Substitute goods

Substitute goods are in competitive demand. For example, a rise in the price of coffee may cause an increase in demand for tea. *XED* is positive for substitute goods, as the two variables of price and demand move in the same direction. There is a positive gradient.

Complementary goods

Complementary goods are in joint demand. They tend to be consumed together. For example, a fall in the price of tennis rackets may cause an increase in demand for tennis balls. *XED* is negative for complementary goods, as the two variables of price and demand move in opposite directions. There is a negative gradient.

Unrelated goods

Unrelated goods have an *XED* value of zero. For example, an increase in the price of cars will have no effect upon the demand for potatoes.

Figure 12 demonstrates cross elasticity of demand for complementary goods and substitute goods.

> **Knowledge check 15**
>
> Distinguish between complementary and substitute goods.

> **Exam tip**
>
> A cross elasticity of demand of zero means there is no relationship between the goods, such as a chocolate bar and beef.

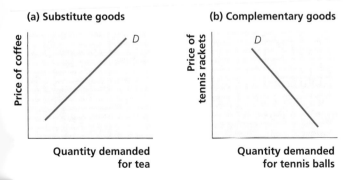

(a) Substitute goods — Price of coffee / Quantity demanded for tea — D

(b) Complementary goods — Price of tennis rackets / Quantity demanded for tennis balls — D

Figure 12 Cross elasticity of demand

Supply

The sellers or producers in a market are said to supply goods and services. **Supply** refers to the quantity of a good or service that firms are willing to sell at a given price and over a given period of time.

An upward-sloping supply curve

A **supply curve** is the quantity of a good or service that firms are willing to sell to a market over a range of different price levels in a given period of time. The supply curve slopes upwards from left to right since: as firms raise output in the short run, they face rising production costs and so pass these costs on to consumers by charging higher prices. Furthermore, as price rises, it encourages firms to supply more of a good to increase profits. Indeed, higher prices may encourage firms to enter a market and so raise supply.

The market supply curve is the horizontal summation of individual firms' supply curves for a particular good or service.

Movement along a supply curve

There is movement along a supply curve for a good only when there is a change in its price. A rise in price causes an extension in supply, and a fall in price causes a contraction in supply, as shown in Figure 13.

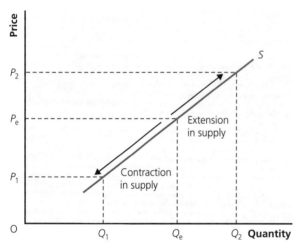

Figure 13 Movement along a supply curve

Shifts in the supply curve

An increase in supply refers to the whole supply curve shifting outwards to the right at every price level (to S_2 in Figure 14). A decrease in supply refers to the whole supply curve shifting inwards to the left at every price level (to S_1 in Figure 14).

Supply The quantity of a good or service that firms are willing to sell at a given price and over a given period of time.

Supply curve Shows the quantity of a good or service that firms are willing to sell to a market over a range of different price levels in a given period of time.

Knowledge check 16

Why does the supply curve slope upwards from left to right?

Knowledge check 17

What causes a movement along a supply curve for a good?

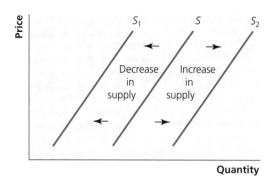

Figure 14 Shifts in the supply curve

There are various factors that can shift the supply curve of a good. For example, the supply of oil could increase due to:

- improvements in technology (e.g. the development of hydraulic fracturing techniques to extract oil from shale rock deposits — known as fracking)
- a reduction in labour costs (e.g. lower wages for oil platform and oil refinery workers)
- a reduction in capital costs (e.g. oil platforms, pipelines and refineries)
- a reduction in transport costs (e.g. an increase in the size of oil tankers)
- discovery of new oil fields (e.g. in the Falklands and Uganda)
- an increase in the number of firms in the oil industry
- a decrease in the market influences of OPEC (Organisation of Petroleum Exporting Countries), a producer cartel (this may occur if individual member states decide to produce more than the agreed oil quotas)
- good weather making it easier to extract oil from Alaska or under the sea bed
- a reduction in indirect taxation on oil
- an increase in government subsidies to oil producers

Price elasticity of supply

Price elasticity of supply (*PES*) is the responsiveness of the supply of a good to a change in its price. The formula to calculate *PES* is:

$$PES = \frac{\text{percentage change in supply of a good}}{\text{percentage change in price of a good}}$$

In most cases a positive answer is obtained, indicating that the two variables of price and quantity move in the same direction. There is a positive gradient.

If *PES* is greater than 1, the good is relatively price elastic: that is, the percentage change in supply is greater than the percentage change in price of the good.

If *PES* is less than 1, the good is relatively price inelastic: that is, the percentage change in supply is less than the percentage change in price of the good.

If *PES* is equal to 1, the good is unit elastic: that is, the percentage change in supply is the same as the percentage change in price of the good.

Exam tip

A change in price of a good will lead to a movement along the supply curve for that particular good; it will not shift the supply curve.

Knowledge check 18

What causes a shift in the supply curve for a good?

Price elasticity of supply The responsiveness of the supply of a good or service to a change in its price.

Knowledge check 19

What does a positive figure mean in price elasticity of supply answers?

If *PES* is equal to zero, the good is perfectly inelastic: that is, a change in price has no effect on the quantity supplied. The supply curve is vertical.

If *PES* is infinite, the good is perfectly elastic. The supply curve is horizontal.

Figure 15 shows the different price elasticities of supply.

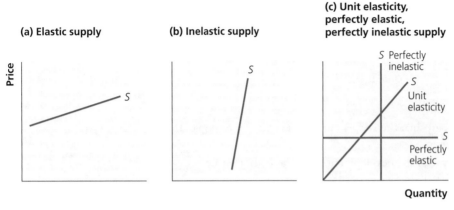

Figure 15 Different price elasticities of supply

Knowledge check 20

What does the 'number' represent in price elasticity of supply answers?

Determinants of price elasticity of supply

- *Level of spare capacity.* A high level of spare capacity in a firm means that it can raise production quickly, so supply tends to be elastic. A firm or industry operating at full capacity is unable to raise output quickly and so its supply tends to be price inelastic.
- *State of the economy.* In a recession there are many unemployed resources and so there is a high level of spare capacity. Firms find it relatively easy to raise supply if needed.
- *Level of stocks of finished goods in a firm.* A high level of stocks means that the firm can increase supply quickly, so supply is price elastic: for example, US motor vehicle manufacturers often have stockpiles of cars waiting to sell. Alternatively, a firm or industry operating with low stocks is unable to raise output quickly and so supply tends to be price inelastic. This is more likely to be the case for a firm making designer wedding dresses.
- *Perishability of the product.* Some goods cannot be stockpiled: for example, some agricultural goods such as fresh fruit, vegetables and flowers are highly perishable. These goods are typically price inelastic in supply. On the other hand, manufactured goods tend to be non-perishable and so can be stockpiled by firms in order to meet anticipated increases in demand. Examples are household electrical goods such as fridges, freezers and washing machines.
- *Ease of entry to an industry.* If there are high entry barriers to an industry then it will be difficult for new firms to enter, even with the attraction of high prices and profits. Sometimes existing producers deliberately create entry barriers, so supply may be restricted and inelastic. Entry barriers include high levels of expenditure on advertising and branding of goods, discouraging new firms from setting up in the market.

■ *Time period under consideration.* Supply tends to be relatively price inelastic in the short run. The short run is the period of time in which a firm is able to increase supply with its existing capacity. At least one factor input is likely to be fixed in quantity in the short run, which makes it difficult for a firm to raise production. However, supply is likely to be relatively price elastic in the long run. The long run is the period of time in which a firm is able to increase supply by adding to its production capacity. All factor inputs are variable in the long run, making it easier for a firm to raise production.

Exam tip

Be careful not to confuse the determinants of price elasticity of supply with those of price elasticity of demand. This is one of the most common mistakes that examiners encounter when marking elasticity of supply questions.

For many agricultural products, supply is price inelastic in the short run because the output from the summer and autumn harvests depends on the amount of seed planted at the start of the year. It takes an even longer period of time to raise the supply of products from livestock, such as milk and beef, because these depend on the nurturing of animals over several years.

The supply of minerals may also be price inelastic in the short run due to the length of time required to explore and discover new deposits and then extract them. The costs and technical complexities involved could be phenomenal. For example, developing a new iron ore mine in Western Australia, to cater for increasing demand from China, will require heavy machinery and the construction of new rail and road links. Mining companies often allow a ten-year period from exploration and development through to commercial extraction of a mineral.

Knowledge check 21

How might the price elasticity of supply for a good change over time?

Exam tip

Be prepared to draw a diagram to show how price elasticity of supply may vary over time to support your answer (see Figure 16).

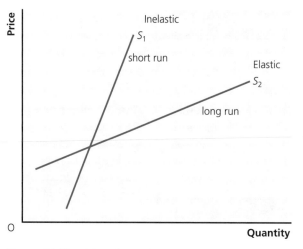

Figure 16 Elasticity of supply

Summary

- Economists assume that consumers and producers make rational decisions: this means consumers spend their income to maximise utility and producers allocate their resources to maximise profits.
- A movement along a demand curve is caused by a change in the price of the good, whereas a shift in a demand curve is caused by changes in real income, tastes, and the price of substitutes and complementary goods.
- The downward-sloping demand curve can be explained by diminishing marginal utility. As additional units of a good are consumed, marginal utility falls, so consumers will only buy more of a product as its price falls.
- A change in the price of a good towards unitary elasticity of demand will lead to an increase in total revenue.
- The determinants of price elasticity of demand for a good include the availability of substitutes, the proportion of income spent on it, the time period and whether it is addictive.
- Normal goods have a positive and inferior goods a negative income elasticity of demand.
- Substitute goods have a positive and complementary goods a negative cross elasticity of demand.
- A movement along a supply curve is caused by a change in the price of the good, whereas shifts in a supply curve are caused by other factors: for example, changes in costs of production, technology, the ability of firms to enter and exit an industry, indirect taxes and government subsidies.
- The determinants of price elasticity of supply of a good include the level of spare capacity, state of the economy, level of stocks, perishability, ease of entry and exit to an industry, and time period under consideration.
- A vertical supply curve indicates that supply of a good is perfectly price inelastic: for example, the capacity of Wembley stadium is 90,000 seats.

Price determination

Price is determined through the interaction of demand and supply in a competitive market. An **equilibrium price** and quantity occurs when there is a balance in the market. There is no tendency for price or quantity to change. The equilibrium price and quantity of a good are obtained from the point of intersection between the demand and supply curves. In the table below and Figure 17, the equilibrium price is £80 per unit and the quantity is 30 units per week.

Equilibrium price
The price where the quantity demanded equals the quantity supplied for a good or service in a market.

Price (£)	Quantity demanded per week	Quantity supplied per week
100	10	50
90	20	40
80	30	30
70	40	20
60	50	10

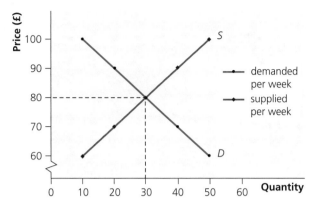

Figure 17 Market equilibrium

Excess supply and excess demand

In a free market, price cannot remain above or below the equilibrium position for long. For example, at a price of £100 there is an **excess supply** of 40 units. In order to sell the surplus, producers tend to reduce price and this encourages consumers to buy more. Demand extends and supply contracts until the equilibrium price of £80 is reached.

At a price of £60 there is an **excess demand** of 40 units. Consumers tend to bid up the price in order to obtain the good and this encourages producers to supply more. Supply extends and demand contracts until the equilibrium price of £80 is reached. Thus, the price mechanism automatically eliminates surpluses and shortages of a good — something that the economist Adam Smith referred to as the 'invisible hand' of the market.

Functions of the price mechanism

Price is the exchange value of a good or service. The **price mechanism** refers to the way price responds to changes in demand or supply for a product or factor input, so that a new equilibrium position is reached in a market. It is the principal method of allocating resources in a market economy. The price mechanism has several functions:

■ *A rationing device.* Resources are scarce, which means that the goods and services produced from them are limited in supply. The price mechanism allocates these goods and services to those who are prepared to pay the most for them. In effect, price will rise or fall until equilibrium is reached between the quantity demanded and quantity supplied.

■ *An incentive device.* Rising prices tend to act as an incentive to firms to produce more of a good or service, since higher profits can be earned. Rising prices also mean firms are able to cover the extra costs involved with increasing output.

■ *A signalling device.* The price mechanism indicates changes in the conditions of demand or supply. For example, an increase in demand for a good or service raises its price and encourages firms to expand their supply, while a decrease in demand lowers the price and causes firms to contract their supply. Consequently, more or fewer resources are allocated to the production of a particular good or service.

Excess supply Where the quantity supplied exceeds the quantity demanded for a good at the current market price.

Knowledge check 22

What is likely to happen to the price of a good if supply exceeds demand in a free market?

Excess demand Where the quantity demanded exceeds the quantity supplied for a good at the current market price.

Knowledge check 23

What is likely to happen to the price of a good if demand exceeds supply in a free market?

Price mechanism The use of market forces to allocate resources in order to solve the economic problem of what, how and for whom to produce.

Any of the factors which may shift demand or supply curves will lead to a change in price of a good or service.

> **Exam tip**
>
> The most effective way to explain the functions of the price mechanism is by using a demand and supply diagram. For example, an increase in demand for gold will raise its price and offer a profit incentive for more to be supplied to the market. The rise in price also acts as a signal to the market for more to be produced.

Consumer and producer surplus

Consumer surplus is the extra amount of money consumers are prepared to pay for a good or service above what they actually pay. It is the utility or satisfaction gained from a good or service in excess of the amount paid for it.

Producer surplus is the extra amount of money paid to producers above what they are willing to accept to supply a good or service. It is the extra earnings obtained by a producer above the minimum required for them to supply the good or service.

The areas of consumer and producer surplus are shown in Figure 18. Consumer surplus is the area above the equilibrium price but below the demand curve; producer surplus is the area below the equilibrium price and above the supply curve.

Consumer surplus The extra amount of money consumers are prepared to pay for a good or service above what they actually pay.

Producer surplus The extra amount of money paid to producers above what they are willing to accept to supply a good or service.

> **Exam tip**
>
> When labelling diagrams, do not confuse consumer surplus with consumer subsidy, or producer surplus with producer subsidy. These are common mistakes made by students.

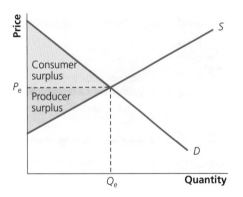

Figure 18 Consumer and producer surplus

The impact of an increase in demand on producer surplus and consumer surplus

An increase in demand for a good is likely to raise producer surplus and consumer surplus (assuming all other things remain equal). In Figure 19, demand increases from D to D_1, causing the equilibrium price to rise from P_e to P_1. Producer surplus increases from BXP_e to BYP_1. The actual rise in producer surplus is area P_eXYP_1. Consumer surplus will also increase from area AXP_e to VYP_1.

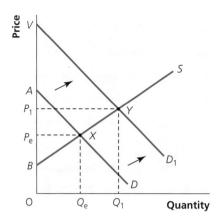

Figure 19 Impact of an increase in demand on consumer surplus and producer surplus

The impact of a decrease in supply on consumer surplus and producer surplus

A decrease in supply of a good is likely to reduce consumer surplus and producer surplus. In Figure 20, supply decreases from S to S_1, causing the equilibrium price to rise from P_e to P_1. Consumer surplus decreases from area AXP_e to AWP_1. The actual loss in consumer surplus is area WXP_eP_1. Producer surplus will also decrease from area BXP_e to GWP_1.

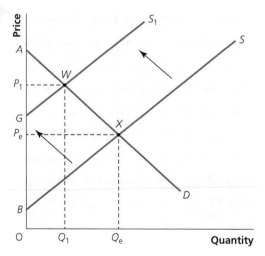

Figure 20 Impact of a decrease in supply on consumer surplus and producer surplus

Exam tip

For short-answer questions on consumer surplus or producer surplus, where a diagram is provided, you should always state the original area, the new area and the actual increase or decrease in area. This could be done by annotating the diagram.

Knowledge check 24

Briefly explain how a decrease in demand for a good affects producer surplus and consumer surplus.

Exam tip

Do not assume that a fall in the price of a good will automatically increase consumer surplus. It depends on the reason for the fall in price. For example, a decrease in the demand for a good will lead to a lower price and lower consumer surplus.

Knowledge check 25

Briefly explain how a decrease in supply of a good affects consumer surplus and producer surplus.

Exam tip

Do not assume that a rise in the price of a good will automatically increase producer surplus. It depends on the reason for the rise in price. For example, a decrease in the supply of a good will lead to a rise in price but a lower producer surplus.

Indirect taxes

A tax is a compulsory charge made by the government on goods, services, incomes or capital. The purpose is to raise funds to pay for government spending programmes. There are two types of tax: direct and indirect.

A direct tax is levied directly on an individual or organisation. Direct taxes are generally paid on incomes: for example, personal income tax and corporation tax (on company profits).

An **indirect tax** is usually levied on the purchase of goods and services. It represents a tax on expenditure. There are two types of indirect tax: specific and *ad valorem* taxes. A specific tax is charged as a fixed amount per unit of a good, such as a litre of wine or a packet of cigarettes. An excise tax is a good example. An *ad valorem* tax is charged as a percentage of the price of a good: for example, VAT of 20% is added on to restaurant meals.

The imposition of an indirect tax raises the price of a good or service. The tax is added to the supply price, effectively causing the supply curve to shift vertically upwards and to the left (a decrease in supply). A specific tax causes a parallel shift of the supply curve to the left, as shown in part (a) of Figure 21. An *ad valorem* tax causes a pivotal rotation of the supply curve to the left, as shown in part (b).

Indirect tax A tax imposed on goods or services supplied by businesses. It includes both specific and *ad valorem* taxes.

Knowledge check 26

Distinguish between a specific tax and an *ad valorem* tax.

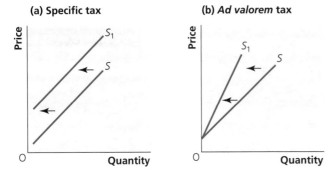

Figure 21 Specific tax and *ad valorem* tax

The incidence of an indirect tax

The **incidence of a tax** usually falls partly on consumers and partly on producers, depending on the relative price elasticities of demand and supply for the good or service. A combination of price inelastic demand and price elastic supply tends to place most of the tax burden on consumers; addictive goods such as tobacco and alcohol tend to be price inelastic in demand. This means that firms are able to pass most of the burden of tax on to consumers via higher prices.

However, a combination of price elastic demand and price inelastic supply tends to place most of the tax burden on the producers. It may also lead to a significant reduction in output and employment. Consequently, a government may be reluctant to place high indirect taxes on these types of goods or services.

Figure 22 shows the effects of a specific tax on a good. Before the tax, the equilibrium price is P_e and quantity Q_e. After the tax is imposed, the supply curve shifts to S_1 and the equilibrium price rises to P_1 while quantity falls to Q_1. The total tax area is $XYWP_1$.

Incidence of tax The distribution of the tax paid between consumers and producers.

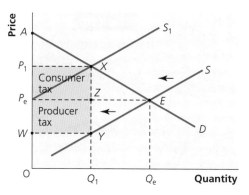

Figure 22 The incidence of taxation

The incidence of tax paid by consumers is shown by the actual rise in market price from P_e to P_1. Consumers pay the amount of tax shown by the area XZP_eP_1. The tax paid by producers is the remaining area $ZYWP_e$.

There is a welfare loss from the specific tax shown by the area XEY. This is the part of the loss of consumer and producer surplus which is not transferred to the government in tax. It is a loss of welfare to society.

Subsidies

A **subsidy** is a grant, usually provided by the government, to encourage suppliers to increase production of a good or service, leading to a fall in its price. Bus and train companies are often given subsidies in order to increase the number of bus and train services, which benefits both the firms and consumers.

A subsidy is often paid directly to producers, but as they respond by increasing output, the market price falls and this indirectly passes on some of the gain to consumers. If demand is price inelastic, then the market price falls by a relatively large amount, increasing the benefits to consumers. If demand is price elastic, then market price falls by a relatively small amount and so there is less gain for consumers. Figure 23 shows the imposition of a government subsidy for a good.

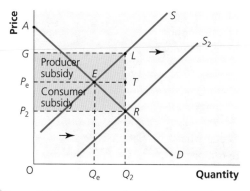

Figure 23 A government subsidy to producers

Before the subsidy, equilibrium price is P_e and Q_e. After the subsidy is imposed, the supply curve shifts to S_2 and equilibrium price falls to P_2 while the quantity rises to Q_2. The total subsidy area is $RLGP_2$.

The amount of subsidy that consumers gain is shown by the actual fall in market price from P_e to P_2. They gain by paying a lower price for the good. The consumer subsidy area is RTP_eP_2. The remaining subsidy area of $TLGP_e$ represents the gain made by producers.

> **Exam tip**
>
> To show a subsidy on a diagram, always start from the *new* equilibrium price position and then draw a vertical line up to the original supply curve. In Figure 23 the starting point is R, and the line is drawn up to L. Many students make the mistake of starting from the original equilibrium price position (shown as E) and then end up with the wrong subsidy area.

Alternative views of consumer behaviour

Economists often assume that consumers behave in a rational manner and so allocate their income to buy goods and services to maximise their utility or satisfaction. (Note that some income may also be saved for future use if the utility gained is greater than current spending on extra items.) Rational economic decision making comes from a deductive approach to the subject, where models are created on the basis of how consumers are *expected* to behave and that their aim *should* be to maximise total utility.

However, an inductive approach to economics starts by investigating how consumers *actually* behave and then develops models from the results. This alternative view of consumer behaviour attempts to explain why they may not always make rational economic decisions. Indeed, consumers may be considered irrational in seeking a *satisfactory* level of utility rather than *maximising* utility. There are several factors which help to explain this behaviour, and these are considered in the following sections.

The influence of other people's behaviour

Consumers are influenced by the behaviour of others: for example, if some people start buying a share in a particular company, others may follow, despite this causing the price to rise and making the share less of a bargain. This 'herd like' mentality is often displayed in various markets where it has become clear that consumers who come late to the market receive little benefit. Property markets offer a reminder of how consumers could lose out by purchasing at the peak of an economic cycle, only to see asset values crash in a downturn.

The importance of habitual behaviour

Habitual behaviour shows itself in two ways:
- *Preference for the status quo.* Consumers are creatures of habit and prefer what they know and have, rather than risking something new where there is more uncertainty: for example, switching bank accounts to get lower charges or switching energy supplier to get lower gas and electricity prices. This consumer inertia could also be explained by the difficulties involved in changing bank or energy supplier — there may be mistakes in the final bills and switchover, and considerable time may be wasted in filling out forms. It appears that for some consumers, doing nothing is preferred to obtaining better deals.

Exam tip

One way of working out the part of a subsidy that is gained by consumers is to consider the actual fall in market price once the subsidy is applied. The fall in market price is the part of the subsidy from which consumers directly benefit; the rest of the subsidy remains with producers.

Knowledge check 27

How does a unit subsidy affect the market price and output for a good?

Knowledge check 28

What is meant by alternative views of consumer behaviour?

■ *Thinking short term.* Consumers are often unrealistic about their future behaviour. For example, many adults are overweight and yet continue their habit of eating too much. This is because they expect to change their habit and eat less in the near future. However, often they do not eat less and so remain overweight, leading to long-term health problems. This is a case of overvaluing the utility from eating too much today and undervaluing the utility of being thinner and having fewer health problems in the future.

Consumer weakness at computation

There are also two aspects to this:

■ *Limited processing skills.* Many consumers have difficulty in calculating the best buys: for example, when shopping at a supermarket and facing a choice of different-sized packs of the same good — the larger size is not always the cheapest per unit. Consumers may simply lack the mathematical skills required to calculate the best buy.

■ *Imperfect market knowledge.* This often underlies the weakness that some consumers display in computation. Consumers may buy a good at a higher price than necessary or a good of lower quality since they do not have full market knowledge on which to base their decisions. It means markets may operate inefficiently, a theme investigated in the next section.

Knowledge check 29

Outline three reasons why consumers may not maximise total utility.

Summary

■ In a competitive market, the equilibrium price and quantity of a good or service is determined by the interaction of demand and supply.
■ The price mechanism is the use of market forces to allocate resources in order to solve the economic problem of what, how and for whom to produce. Its three functions are to operate as a rationing, incentive and signalling device in the market.
■ Consumer surplus is the utility or satisfaction gained from a good or service in excess of the price paid for it. Producer surplus is the extra earnings obtained by a producer above the minimum required for them to supply the good or service.
■ An excess demand for a good will cause price to rise until equilibrium is reached; an excess supply of a good will cause price to fall until equilibrium is reached.
■ An indirect tax on a good will cause an inward shift in the supply curve, leading to a fall in output and a rise in price.
■ A unit subsidy on a good will cause an outward shift in the supply curve, leading to a rise in output and a fall in price.
■ Alternative views of consumer behaviour are based on real-world investigations of how consumers actually behave. This indicates that consumers may not aim to maximise total utility, or they may be confused over the behaviour required to do this.

■ Market failure

Types of market failure

Market failure occurs when the price mechanism causes an inefficient allocation of resources and so leads to a net welfare loss. Consequently, resources are not allocated to their best or optimum use.

There are various types of market failure and you may come across different classifications in your textbooks. However, Theme 1 of the specification focuses on the following: externalities, under-provision of public goods and information gaps. Each of these is now considered in turn.

Externalities

Externalities are those costs or benefits which are external to an exchange. They are third-party effects ignored by the price mechanism.

Externalities are also known as *indirect costs* and *benefits*, or as *spillovers from production* or *consumption* of a good or service. In effect, external costs are *negative externalities* and external benefits are *positive externalities*.

External costs

External costs may occur in the production and the consumption of a good or service. An example of an external cost in production is a chemical firm polluting a river with its waste. This causes an external cost to the fishing and water supply industries. Fish catches may be reduced and it may become very expensive to purify water to meet the European Commission's safety standards.

An example of an external cost in consumption is a person smoking tobacco, polluting the air for others. The effect is to cause passive smoking, where non-smokers may suffer the same illnesses as smokers.

Private costs

In a free market, producers are only concerned with the **private costs** of production. These are costs internal to the firm, which it pays for directly. These costs include wages for workers, rent of buildings, payment for raw materials, machinery costs, electricity and gas costs, insurance, packaging and transport costs from running lorries. Private costs may also refer to the market price that a consumer pays for a good or service.

Social costs

By adding private costs to external costs, we obtain **social costs**. This means that external costs are the difference between private costs and social costs. The marginal private cost and marginal social cost curves often diverge, indicating that external costs increase disproportionately with output. However, it is possible that external costs per unit of output remain constant, in which case the marginal private cost and marginal social cost curves are drawn parallel to each other. The relationship between private cost, external cost and social cost is shown in Figure 24.

Market failure When the price mechanism causes an inefficient allocation of resources, leading to a net welfare loss.

External costs Negative third-party effects outside of a market transaction.

Exam tip

When defining external costs, offer two ideas as there are often 2 marks available: for example, 'They are negative third-party effects and represent costs outside of the market transaction.' Also be prepared to give an example, such as pollution from coal extraction or gas fracking.

Private costs Costs internal to a market transaction, which are therefore taken into account by the price mechanism.

Social costs The sum of external costs and private costs from a market transaction.

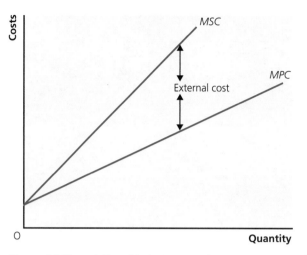

Figure 24 The relationship between private cost, external cost and social cost in the production of a good

Note that the Edexcel specification focuses on diagrammatic analysis of external costs in production.

External benefits

External benefits may occur in the production and consumption of a good or service. An example of an external benefit in production is the recycling of waste materials such as newspapers, glass and tins. It has the benefit of reducing the amount of waste disposal for landfill sites as well as re-using materials for production. It helps to promote sustainable economic growth.

An external benefit in consumption is the vaccination of an individual against various diseases. It reduces the possibility of other people catching a disease who come into contact with the vaccinated individual.

Private benefits

In a free market, consumers are only concerned with the **private benefits** or utility from consuming a good or service. Economists assume this can be measured by the price that consumers are prepared to pay for a good or service. Private benefits may also refer to the revenue that a firm obtains from selling a good or service.

Social benefits

By adding private benefits to external benefits, we obtain **social benefits**. This means external benefits are the difference between private benefits and social benefits. The marginal private benefit and marginal social benefit curves often diverge, indicating that external benefits increase disproportionately with output consumed, as shown in Figure 25. However, it is possible that external benefit per unit consumed will remain constant, in which case the marginal private benefit and marginal social benefit curves are drawn parallel to each other.

Knowledge check 30

What are social costs?

External benefits
Positive third-party effects outside of a market transaction.

Exam tip

When defining external benefits, offer two ideas as there are often 2 marks available: for example, 'They are positive third-party effects and represent benefits outside of the market transaction.' Also be prepared to give an example, such as increased house prices for homeowners near an urban regeneration scheme.

Private benefits
Benefits internal to a market transaction, which are therefore taken into account by the price mechanism.

Social benefits The sum of external benefits and private benefits from a market transaction.

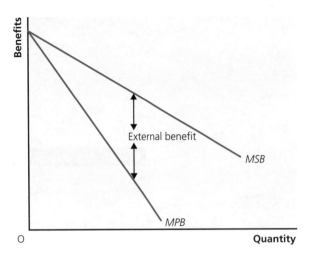

Figure 25 The private benefits, external benefits and social benefits from the consumption of a good

Knowledge check 31

What are social benefits?

Note that the Edexcel specification focuses on diagrammatic analysis of external benefits in consumption of goods and services.

Table 1 Examples of external costs and external benefits

	External costs	External benefits
Production	■ A waste disposal firm dumping toxic waste at sea, which destroys fish life. ■ Burning coal in power stations to create electricity, adding to global warming. ■ Increased production of biofuels, which destroy rain forests and increase food prices.	■ A paper and glass recycling plant, which reduces the waste for landfill sites. ■ Construction of the London Crossrail project, increasing inward investment and raising local property prices. ■ The use of wind turbines and tidal power to create electricity. These are renewable forms of energy, which emit less carbon emissions than fossil fuels.
Consumption	■ Excess alcohol intake, which leads to vandalism. ■ Increased road congestion around the expansion of Heathrow airport. ■ Tobacco smoking, which affects passive smokers.	■ Education and training programmes, which increase human capital levels. Higher labour productivity increases profits for firms. ■ Improving the quality of one's garden, which increases the value of neighbouring houses. ■ The consumption of vaccinations, which help reduce the spread of diseases and so increase life expectancy for millions.

The free market equilibrium

The supply curve for a firm is the marginal private cost curve (MPC). The addition of all the MPC curves of firms in a market for a particular good or service will form the market supply curve.

The demand curve for consumers is the marginal private benefit curve (MPB). Economists assume that it is possible to measure the benefit obtained from consuming a good by the price people are prepared to pay for it. As an individual consumes more units of a good, the marginal benefit (marginal utility) will fall. This is why the demand curve slopes downwards from left to right. The addition of all the consumers' MPB curves for a particular good or service will form the market demand curve.

Market equilibrium occurs at the price and output position where marginal private benefit equals marginal private cost.

Market equilibrium
Where marginal private benefit equals marginal private cost.

The social optimum equilibrium

The social optimum equilibrium level of output or price for a good or service occurs where marginal social cost (MSC) equals marginal social benefit (MSB). The social cost of producing the last unit of output equals the social benefit from consuming it. When the social optimum is reached in a market, welfare is maximised.

Social optimum Where marginal social benefit equals marginal social cost.

External costs and the triangle of welfare loss

The free market ignores negative externalities. However, adding external costs on to the production of a good or service, such as the production of chemical goods, causes the supply curve of the firm to shift to the left and become the marginal social cost curve, shown in Figure 26.

Knowledge check 32

Distinguish between the market equilibrium and social optimum positions in a market.

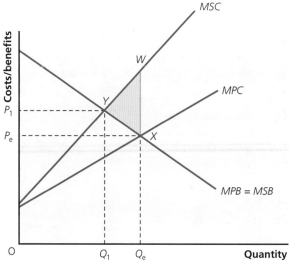

Note: for simplicity we have assumed there are no external benefits

Figure 26 External costs and the triangle of welfare loss

Assuming there are no external benefits in the production of a chemical good, the social optimum equilibrium is at price OP_1 and quantity OQ_1. When external costs are ignored, there is underpricing and overproduction. There is an excess of social costs over social benefits for the marginal output between Q_e and Q_1.

The marginal social cost of the output slice Q_eQ_1 is Q_eWYQ_1, which exceeds the marginal social benefit of this output, Q_eXYQ_1. The excess of social costs over social benefits is shown by the triangle XWY. This is the area of welfare loss to society; the market has failed, since negative externalities are ignored.

Knowledge check 33

What is the triangle of welfare loss?

External benefits and the triangle of welfare gain

The free market ignores positive externalities. However, adding external benefits on to the consumption of a good or service, such as the consumption of vaccinations, causes the demand curve to shift to the right and become the marginal social benefit curve, shown in Figure 27.

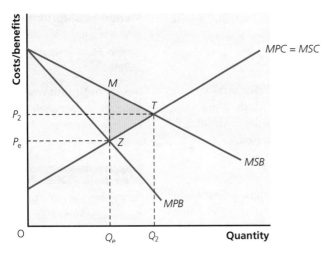

Figure 27 External benefits and the triangle of welfare gain

Assuming there are no external costs in the consumption of vaccinations in a free market, the social optimum equilibrium is at OP_2 and quantity OQ_2. When external benefits are ignored, there is underpricing and underconsumption. There is an excess of social benefits over social costs for the marginal output between Q_e and Q_2. Thus, by raising output from OQ_e to OQ_2, welfare could be increased.

The marginal social benefit of the output slice Q_eQ_2 is Q_eMTQ_2, which exceeds the marginal social cost of this output, Q_eZTQ_2. The excess of social benefits over social costs is shown by the triangle MTZ. This is the area of welfare gain to society; the market has failed, since positive externalities are ignored.

The impact of external costs on consumers and producers

External costs can be ignored by consumers and producers when they make their economic decisions, so causing market failure. This leads to:

- Overproduction, since the free market level of output exceeds the social optimum level of output.
- Underpricing, since the free market price is below the social optimum price.
- Welfare loss, since marginal social costs exceed marginal social benefits.
- Concerns over the availability of resources for future generations. For example, overfishing will lead to a collapse in fish stocks, which may become unsustainable.
- Concerns over pollution levels. For example, burning fossil fuels to produce energy could lead to global warming and consequent problems of climate change. Air pollution could also increase respiratory diseases and reduce life expectancy.
- Calls for government intervention to internalise the external costs and so correct market failure. This may take the form of indirect taxes and trade pollution permits (refer to the section 'Government intervention', starting on page 44).

The impact of external benefits on consumers and producers

External benefits can be ignored by consumers and producers making their economic decisions and so cause market failure. This leads to:

Knowledge check 34

What is the triangle of welfare gain?

Exam tip

When inserting the area of welfare loss or welfare gain on an externality diagram, always start from the free market equilibrium position and draw a line vertically up to the *MSC* or *MSB* curve. This will help delineate the area to shade in.

Knowledge check 35

Why do external costs cause market failure?

- Underproduction, since the free market level of output is less than the social optimum level of output.
- Underpricing, since the free market price is below the social optimum price. (Note that society should be prepared to pay more for the goods or services to take account of external benefits.)
- Potential welfare gain, since marginal social benefits exceed marginal social costs.
- Concerns over the long-term implications of underproduction. For example, under-provision of education and healthcare could lead to lower economic growth and a less competitive economy. Living standards may rise more slowly.
- Calls for government intervention to internalise the external benefits and so correct market failure. This may take the form of regulation, government provision and subsidies (see the section 'Government intervention').

Public goods

Some goods may not be produced at all through the markets, despite offering significant benefits to society. Where this occurs it is known as a 'missing market' and the goods are called **public goods**. These goods involve a large element of collective consumption: for example, national defence, flood defence systems, the criminal justice system and refuse collection.

Public goods demonstrate characteristics of non-excludability and non-rivalry.

- Non-excludability means that once a good has been produced for the benefit of one person, it is impossible to stop others from benefiting.
- Non-rivalry means that as more people consume a good and enjoy its benefits, it does not reduce the amount available for others. In effect, it is non-diminishable.

Once a public good has been provided, the cost of supplying it to an extra consumer is zero. Further examples include public firework displays, lighthouses, public beaches, public parks, drains and street lighting.

Note that some goods display non-excludability and non-rivalry in their provision for part of the time, such as roads at off-peak times. However, during peak times there is fierce rivalry for road space. These are known as quasi-public goods.

Private goods

Private goods are the opposite of public goods. They display characteristics of rivalry and excludability in consumption. An example of a private good is a Mars bar, the consumption of which directly excludes other people from consuming that particular bar. The owners of private goods are able to use private property rights which prevent other people from consuming them. Private goods can also be rejected, which means one has a choice over whether to consume them or not.

The free-rider problem

In a free market economy, public goods are under-provided due to the free-rider problem. Once a public good has been provided for one individual, it is automatically provided for all. The market fails because it is not possible for firms to withhold the good from those consumers who refuse to pay for it. Examples are national defence and street pavements.

Knowledge check 36
Why do external benefits cause market failure?

Public goods
Those goods that have non-rivalry and non-excludability in their consumption.

Exam tip
Do not confuse public goods with public expenditure. Public expenditure is government spending in the economy, which may be on consumer goods, capital goods or transfer payments.

Knowledge check 37
When might a public beach cease to be a public good?

Private goods Those goods that have rivalry and excludability in their consumption.

Knowledge check 38
What is meant by the free-rider problem?

The rational consumer would wait for someone else to provide the good and then reap the rewards by consuming it for free. However, if everyone waits for others to supply a public good then it may never be provided. The non-excludability characteristic means that the price mechanism cannot develop as free riders will not pay. Firms are reluctant to supply such a good in a free market as it is difficult to gain profits from it. The solution is for government to provide public goods and fund them from general taxation.

Information gaps

Information gaps can lead to market failure due to either consumers or producers having more market knowledge than the other about a particular good or service. It means there is an unequal balance upon which to conduct economic transactions between them. A good example is the second-hand car market discussed later in this section.

Information gaps can also lead to market failure when consumers or producers simply lack perfect knowledge about a particular good or service and so end up making non-rational economic decisions. A good example is the pension market, where people tend to make too few contributions for their retirement. This is also discussed later in this section.

Symmetric information

In competitive markets, it is often assumed that consumers and producers have **symmetric information** when making their economic decisions — that they have access to the same information about a good or service in a market. Assuming that consumers and producers act in a rational way, symmetric information will lead to an efficient allocation of resources. This means consumers will buy a good or service from a producer offering the best deal, taking into account things like price, quality, reliability and after-sales service.

Asymmetric information

In reality, consumers and producers have **asymmetric information** — that is, unequal market knowledge upon which to make their economic decisions — and this could lead to a misallocation of resources.

How imperfect market knowledge may lead to a misallocation of resources

Producer knowledge may exceed consumer knowledge

A second-hand car salesman, for example, may have greater knowledge of the history of vehicles for sale as well as more technical knowledge than consumers. This could lead to a consumer paying too much for a poor-quality car. The fear of buying a defective car tends to reduce the market price for all second-hand cars, even the good-quality ones. Consequently, the losers could be both buyers and sellers, depending on the car sold. This is known as a lemon market and is associated with the work of the economist George Akerlof.

Knowledge check 39

Why do public goods represent a type of market failure?

Information gaps
Where consumers, producers or the government have insufficient knowledge to make rational economic decisions.

Symmetric information Where consumers and producers have access to the same information about a good or service in the market.

Asymmetric information Where consumers and producers have unequal access to information about a good or service in the market.

The solution is to have inspection schemes offered by motoring organisations such as the Automobile Association. It can inspect a car on behalf of consumers to overcome information failure.

Similar problems arise in the market for healthcare, where private doctors may end up over-treating patients in order to increase their profits. This has occurred in some cases of cosmetic surgery. The solution is to have a watchdog body such as the General Medical Council to investigate and prosecute offending practitioners.

Consumer knowledge may exceed producer knowledge

A consumer may purchase an insurance policy, concealing information about himself or simply know more than the insurance company about his intended future actions. This might include having a risky lifestyle. The insurance company may then provide insurance at too low a price or insure someone who might be too risky to insure, and therefore may make a loss. This could lead to insurers exiting the market or refusing to make the payouts due. The solution is to have a watchdog body with powers to investigate and prosecute fraudulent insurance claims.

Imperfect market knowledge means that many people fail to make sufficient contributions to their pension scheme (a scheme to provide an income to people when they retire from work). This reflects the uncertainty surrounding their long-term future circumstances, such as financial outgoings, quality of health and longevity. There is also risk associated with the type of pension scheme entered into, as returns are linked to the performance of the stock market. Given these problems, it is not surprising that many people make so little provision for retirement and end up in poverty in old age. The solution partly involves government intervention which makes it compulsory for workers to contribute to a National Insurance scheme that pays for state pensions.

Knowledge check 40

Why does imperfect market information lead to market failure?

Summary

- There are various forms of market failure: for example, externalities, under-provision of public goods and information gaps.
- External costs and benefits arise due to third-party effects in market transactions that the price mechanism ignores.
- External costs in production lead to a welfare loss triangle as the free market output equilibrium exceeds the social optimum position.
- External benefits in consumption lead to a potential welfare gain triangle as the free market output equilibrium is less than the social optimum position.
- Public goods display characteristics of non-rivalry and non-excludability in consumption.
- Public goods are underprovided or not provided at all in a free market economy due to the free-rider problem.
- Information gaps mean consumers and producers may make economic decisions on buying and selling goods which reduce their welfare. This can be seen in the underconsumption of healthcare, education and pensions, or the overconsumption of tobacco, alcohol and gambling.
- Symmetric information is where consumers and producers have equal access to market knowledge; asymmetric information is where consumers and producers have unequal access to market knowledge.

Government intervention

Government intervention in markets

The UK is a mixed economy, which means both private enterprise and the government allocate resources to solve the economic problem of what, how and for whom to produce. Often the government intervenes where there is market failure and attempts to correct this so that resources are allocated more efficiently.

There are various measures a government could undertake to correct market failure: for example, indirect taxation, subsidies, maximum prices, minimum prices, trade pollution permits, regulation, provision of public goods and provision of market information. The relative merits of each form of intervention are now considered in relation to different types of market failure. Note that the disadvantages of these measures point to the possibility of government failure.

Knowledge check 41

What is the key reason for government intervention in markets?

Indirect taxation

Indirect taxes are taxes levied on the expenditure of goods or services. The government often imposes taxes on goods which have significant external costs, such as petrol, tobacco, alcohol and electricity generated from burning fossil fuels.

Figure 28 shows the market for petrol, including both the marginal private cost curve (MPC) and the marginal social cost curve (MSC). In a free market the equilibrium price is OP_e and the equilibrium quantity OQ_e. However, the social optimum price is OP_1 and the social optimum quantity OQ_1, where marginal social cost (MSC) equals marginal social benefit (MSB) for the last unit produced. The vertical distance ZY represents the external cost (air pollution) for each litre of petrol consumed.

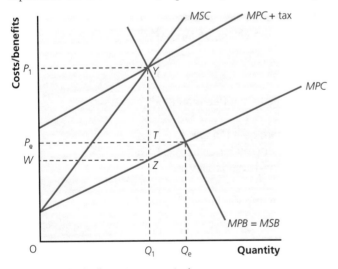

Figure 28 An indirect tax on petrol

By placing a tax equal to the external cost of ZY per litre, the government successfully internalises the pollution. The total tax collected is shown by the area P_1YZW. Both producers and consumers pay the tax, depending on the relative elasticities of demand and supply. The consumer tax area is YP_1P_eT and the producer tax area is P_eTZW.

Knowledge check 42

Why are there high indirect taxes on tobacco, alcohol and petrol?

Advantages of indirect taxes to correct market failure

- In the case of pollution, indirect taxes are based on the principle that the polluters (both producer and consumer) pay, helping to internalise the external costs.
- They work with market forces so that choice still exists in terms of consumption and production, unlike the effects of some regulations. In terms of behavioural economics, this is known as a 'nudge' rather than a 'shove' policy.
- The level of pollution should fall as output of the good or service is reduced and the price increased — the social optimum position of $MSB = MSC$ can be achieved.
- Tax funds are raised for the government and these can be used to clean up the environment or to compensate the victims of pollution.
- Indirect taxes are difficult to evade as they are often included in the market price. The sellers collect the tax revenue and send it to government.
- Indirect taxes are convenient, since they tend to be paid in small amounts and regularly rather than in one lump sum.

Disadvantages of indirect taxes to correct market failure

- It is difficult to quantify external costs and then place a monetary value on them. Consequently, the social optimum position might not be achieved.
- Indirect taxes increase the costs of production for firms, making them less competitive than firms in other countries where such taxes are not applied.
- Widespread use of indirect taxes may be inflationary.
- Firms may relocate to other countries with less stringent taxes on production.
- The demand for the good or service may be price inelastic and so the overall reduction in pollution levels may be small.
- The tax revenue raised may not be used to compensate victims or clean up the environment.
- In the case of some goods, unintended consequences may occur such as the development of illegal markets: for example, tobacco and alcohol smuggling to avoid high taxes.
- The regressive nature of indirect taxes leads to further unintended consequences: for example, the burden of payment tends to fall on low-income rather than high-income groups.

Exam tip

One evaluation technique is to consider the impact on different interest groups: for example, the economic effects of an increase in tax on petrol. This may have a bigger impact on consumers than on petrol producers, since demand is price inelastic. Petrol firms will be able to pass on most of the tax to consumers. The government is also likely to benefit from increased tax revenue.

Subsidies

A subsidy is a grant provided by the government to encourage the production and consumption of a particular good or service. Subsidies are often applied to goods or services with significant external benefits, such as education and healthcare. They may also be given to alternative forms of economic activity which create less pollution, such as public transport and renewable energy.

Figure 29(a) shows the application of a unit subsidy to the market for electricity from renewable energy sources. The effect of the subsidy is to lower the price of each kilowatt of electricity from P_e to P_1 and to increase the quantity from Q_e to Q_1.

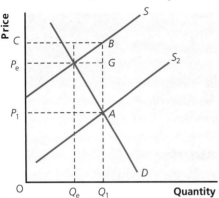
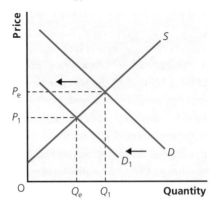

Figure 29 A unit subsidy for renewable electricity generation and the impact on the market for non-renewable electricity generation

The subsidy per unit is AB and the total subsidy area is $ABCP_1$. Part of the subsidy is passed on to consumers in the form of a lower price of electricity, equal to the area AGP_eP_1. The other portion of the subsidy ($GBCP_e$) remains with the producer. The lower price of electricity from renewable energy sources will help decrease the demand for electricity from non-renewable sources from D to D_1 (Figure 29(b)).

Advantages of subsidies applied to renewable energy markets

■ Subsidies can reduce air pollution and other forms of external costs.
■ Subsidies on renewable energy generation promote sustained economic growth.
■ The rate of consumption of non-renewable energy resources is reduced.
■ Subsidies work with market forces and so maintain choice. They help to internalise the external benefits from renewable forms of energy so that the social optimum level of output can be reached.

Disadvantages of subsidies applied to renewable energy markets

■ It is difficult to quantify external benefits and then place a monetary value on them. Consequently, the social optimum position might not be achieved.
■ There is an opportunity cost to government subsidies. They may lead to higher taxes or cuts in government spending elsewhere. They may be a waste of money: for example, many subsidised bus services operate along routes with hardly any passengers.
■ Unintended consequences may occur: for example, firms may become dependent on the subsidies and inefficient in production.
■ Wind power and solar power may be less reliable sources of energy than traditional fossil fuels, leading to possible energy shortages at peak times of use.
■ There are external costs associated with the provision of renewable energy sources: for example, noise and visual pollution from wind farms. They can also reduce property prices nearby.

Knowledge check 43

Why might a government subsidise some goods?

Exam tip

One evaluation technique is to consider the magnitude of an event. For example, when assessing the effects of government subsidies in the renewable energy markets, this will depend upon how large the subsidies are as a proportion of total production costs for firms.

Maximum price schemes

In a **maximum price** scheme, the government may impose a limit on how much prices of certain goods and services can rise. Such schemes have been used in house rental markets to protect tenants from being exploited by their landlords. Similarly, during the Second World War the government imposed maximum prices on basic food items such as milk, eggs and meat (accompanied by ration books for making purchases) to ensure a fairer distribution.

More recently, price caps were applied on various utilities such as gas and electricity. Currently there are price caps on selected rail fares and postal services. There have also been calls for the government to impose maximum wages on exceptionally high-paid public sector workers and bankers. Usually a maximum price is set below the free market price, causing shortages or an excess demand. This is shown in Figure 30 for the private house rental market. Note that a maximum price set above the free market equilibrium price will have no effect.

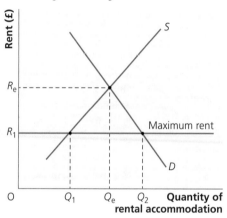

Figure 30 A maximum price scheme

A maximum rent of R_1 causes demand to extend from Q_e to Q_2 and supply to contract from Q_e to Q_1. It leads to an excess demand of Q_1Q_2. The shortage of private rental housing may lead to housing being allocated on a *first-come, first-served* basis or by the *sellers' preference*. Both of these forms of allocation have undesirable consequences. The government may also impose regulations on the type of customers to whom private landlords can rent: for example, vulnerable people or young mothers. However, it is more likely that this type of legislation will be used for public sector housing.

Advantages of maximum prices

- They can reduce exploitation of consumers, especially where a lack of competition exists. For example, the EU has capped the price of some mobile phone calls across member states.
- They can reduce inequality, as in the case of a salary cap on highly paid public sector workers and bankers.
- They can help people on low incomes to afford key products: for example, rental housing.

Maximum price A ceiling price set by the government on a good or service, above which it cannot rise. It may be enforced through government legislation.

Knowledge check 44

Why might a government impose a maximum price in the house rental market?

Disadvantages of maximum prices

- Unintended consequences may occur: for example, government intervention distorts the operation of the price mechanism, leading to an excess demand and inefficient allocation of resources.
- In terms of the house rental market, it reduces the supply of rental property and makes the shortage worse in the long run.
- Producer surplus falls and so landlords have less income with which to invest in and maintain their property.
- Problems arise over how to allocate supply to meet the excess demand in the market, since price cannot increase. This may involve a *first-come, first-served* basis or *sellers' preference* — both of which are deemed to be unfair.
- It is difficult for the government to monitor and enforce maximum price controls in markets. There is a danger of shadow markets being created. Some people may be prepared to pay more for the good to ensure they obtain it. This is often seen with tickets at popular football matches and theatre shows.

Minimum price schemes

In a **minimum price** scheme, the government may impose a limit on how much prices of certain goods and services can fall. Such schemes have been used in commodity markets to protect the income of farmers and also in labour markets to prevent the exploitation of workers (the national minimum wage). More recently, there have been calls for a minimum price on goods which create high external costs, such as alcohol and sugar. In 2018 the Scottish government introduced a minimum price of 50p for each unit of alcohol in order to reduce excessive drinking by some people.

Figure 31 shows the effects of a minimum price scheme in agriculture. For example, EU farmers are guaranteed a minimum price for many commodities, including sugar, wheat and barley. Usually the minimum price is set above the free market price, causing agricultural surpluses or an excess supply. These are purchased by a government agency at the **guaranteed minimum price**. Note that a minimum price set below the free market equilibrium price will have no effect.

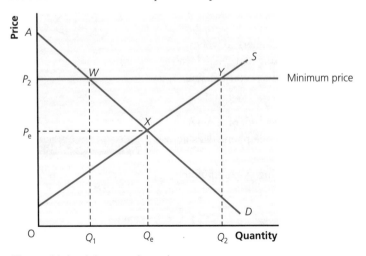

Figure 31 A minimum price scheme

A minimum price of P_2 causes demand to contract from Q_e to Q_1 and supply to extend from Q_e to Q_2. It leads to an excess supply of Q_1Q_2. Government expenditure on the surplus is shown by the area Q_1Q_2YW and total farm revenue increases from OP_eXQ_e to OP_2YQ_2. The excess supply is stockpiled by the government.

Advantages of minimum prices

- They can reduce the consumption of goods which are harmful to consumers and have high external costs, such as alcohol and sugar.
- They encourage producers to switch to making 'healthier' drinks and foods containing less alcohol and sugar.
- They can reduce fluctuations in food prices and so make it easier for consumers to budget their income. They also ensure food supplies even in times of poor harvest, due to the availability of surplus stockpiles.
- A guaranteed minimum price can stabilise and increase producer incomes, leading to greater investment and employment: for example, in agriculture.
- Food surpluses can be used as a form of international aid to developing countries.
- A national minimum wage can reduce exploitation of labour while increasing incentives to work.

Disadvantages of minimum prices

- Unintended consequences may occur: for example, government intervention distorts the operation of the price mechanism, leading to an excess supply and inefficient allocation of resources.
- The price of some food and drinks will increase, which could lead to hardship for consumers on low incomes. A minimum price also reduces consumer surplus.
- Minimum prices may be less effective in reducing consumption of alcohol and sugary drinks when demand is price inelastic.
- A guaranteed minimum price scheme leads to the government buying up (agricultural) surpluses, which involves an opportunity cost. It may have to raise taxes or cut government spending elsewhere.
- There are increased storage and security costs for the food surpluses. Alternatively, the food surpluses may have to be destroyed due to their perishability.
- The food surpluses may be sold in overseas markets at very low prices. This could damage farmers in developing countries, who are unable to compete against imports of cheap food.
- Farmers are guaranteed an income, which might cause them to become less efficient over time. There is less incentive for farmers to improve the quality of the food or to keep production costs down.
- A national minimum wage may cause unemployment among workers in low-skilled labour markets.
- It is difficult for the government to monitor and enforce a minimum wage policy.

Tradable pollution permits

In 2005 the European Commission set up an Emissions Trading System (ETS) in an attempt to limit greenhouse gas emissions from heavy industry. Its main focus is to curb carbon dioxide emissions by major polluters in the European Union, such as the power generators, steel, paper, cement and ceramics industries. The scheme limits

Exam tip

Be prepared to annotate any diagrams provided in the multiple-choice and short-answer questions. This includes identifying the amount of excess supply on a guaranteed minimum price diagram.

Knowledge check 46

Why might a government impose a minimum price for alcoholic drinks and sugar?

Knowledge check 47

What are the disadvantages of imposing a minimum price on alcohol and sugar?

emissions from around 11,000 power plants and manufacturing companies which comprise some 45% of the EU's greenhouse gas emissions. It was intended to include the aviation industry in the scheme in 2012, but objections from countries outside of the EU have delayed its implementation.

The ETS is a 'cap and trade' system. Each year, the European Commission allocates a set amount of carbon dioxide permits to national governments, which then divide up the allowances among the firms covered by the scheme. The system 'caps' the amount of carbon emissions for the year. This cap is reduced by around 1.7% each year. The pollution permits are tradable, which means that firms can buy and sell the allowances between themselves.

Initially, most of the **tradable pollution permits** were given free to industry and allocated on the basis of the amount of pollution created before the scheme was introduced. However, currently just 40% of permits are free, providing more incentive to firms to invest in clean technology and so reduce carbon emissions in the long term. There is also a reserve of carbon permits to enable new firms to enter those industries within the emissions trading scheme. Furthermore, national governments are able to retain up to 10% of permits and offer them for sale, depending on the level of scarcity.

> **Tradable pollution permits** Pollution permits that can be bought and sold in a market. They are an attempt to solve the problem of pollution by creating a market for it.

The ETS also allows firms to invest in schemes that reduce greenhouse gas emissions outside the European Union: for example, in India and China. The savings in carbon emissions can then be offset against their own emissions in the European Union.

The UK is the second largest emitter of greenhouse gases in Europe and its companies are some of the largest buyers of pollution permits.

> **Knowledge check 48**
>
> What is meant by a 'cap and trade' scheme?

Advantages of trade pollution permits

- A market is created for buying and selling carbon permits, just like other goods and services. In effect, the price mechanism is used to internalise the external costs associated with carbon emissions.
- EU pollution permits have been reduced over time as part of a coordinated plan. For example, between 1990 and 2019 the EU has been able to reduce greenhouse gas emissions by more than 20%.
- National governments can raise funds by selling their reserve pollution permits to industry. The revenue could then be used to clean up the environment or compensate victims.
- Firms have an incentive to invest in clean technology.
- Production costs will increase for firms that exceed their pollution allowances, since they have to purchase additional permits, and this provides a source of revenue for cleaner firms that can sell their excess pollution permits.
- The ETS may act as a foundation for a global scheme. It has attracted interest from developed countries outside of the EU. For example, Norway, Iceland and Liechtenstein have joined the scheme whereas the state of California and also north-eastern USA have set up parallel schemes.
- Firms are able to bank their excess pollution permits for use in future years.

> **Knowledge check 49**
>
> Why has the EU introduced a system of tradable pollution permits?

Disadvantages of trade pollution permits

- An information gap might cause the European Commission to issue too many carbon permits, so that there is little incentive for firms to reduce pollution. This occurred during the first phase of the ETS (2005–07) and led to a collapse in the price of carbon allowances. This reflected the absence of a means to bank spare allowances at the time.
- An information gap might cause the European Commission to issue too few carbon permits, so that production costs for EU firms increase rapidly, reducing their international competitiveness. Some firms may even relocate outside of the EU to reduce production costs.
- Disputes have arisen over the allocation of carbon permits to firms. Some companies believe they should receive larger allowances and have taken legal proceedings against the European Commission.
- Firms may pass the costs of purchasing pollution permits on to their customers, leading to higher prices of, for example, electricity, steel, glass and paper. This is more likely to happen if demand is price inelastic.
- Unintended consequences may occur: for example, there is less pressure on major polluting firms to clean up their act if it is possible to buy extra permits from elsewhere.
- EU firms may avoid investing in expensive technology to reduce their own emissions by funding cheaper carbon-offsetting schemes in developing countries.
- The price of pollution permits has fluctuated considerably since their inception in 2005. For example, the price of carbon emissions has varied from over €25 to less than €1 per ton. This has created uncertainty among firms about whether to invest heavily in carbon-reducing technology. Firms need clear guidance on what carbon prices will be for the next decade in order to determine their investment levels.
- There is a cost to the government of monitoring pollution emissions from the many companies within the scheme.
- The EU is just one part of the world. Unless all countries engage in similar carbon trading schemes, global emissions will continue to increase. For example, China is responsible for more than a quarter of all global carbon emissions, being the world's largest polluter, but it is not part of an emissions trading scheme.
- The valuation of pollution permits is an inexact science. Perhaps it is too important to leave to the market. Much disagreement exists over the costs of greenhouse gas emissions. Some environmental groups believe too little is being done to reduce carbon emissions. Carbon trading is simply leading to a false sense of security.

State provision of public goods

It was mentioned earlier that public goods would not be provided (or would be under-provided) in a free market economy due to the free-rider problem. Once the good is provided, people are able to consume it without paying, and so private enterprise has no incentive to supply it, since making a profit would be difficult.

Consequently, the government or state tends to provide public goods in order to correct market failure. It raises funds from general taxation to pay for their provision. This is a major reason why most economies are mixed economies today. Public goods involve a large element of collective consumption: for example, national defence, flood defence systems, the criminal justice system and refuse collection.

Knowledge check 50

How might the success of the EU Emissions Trading System be affected by the number of pollution permits issued?

Exam tip

One evaluation technique is to consider both advantages and disadvantages. For example, a question examining the advantages of tradable carbon permits as a means of reducing pollution invites you to consider the pros and cons of such a scheme.

State provision of information

It was mentioned earlier that information gaps cause market failure and so require government intervention to reduce this. Today, government provision of information comes through various promotions using social media such as the internet, television, radio, newspapers and text messages. The reasons are:

- To encourage the production and consumption of healthy goods and services, for example fruit and vegetables, or goods that yield long-term benefits, such as pensions. Often these are underprovided in the market.
- To discourage the production and consumption of unhealthy goods and services, for example tobacco, alcohol and drugs. Often these are overprovided in the market.
- To notify and remind people of laws for their own protection, such as wearing seatbelts in motor vehicles and not drinking alcohol and driving.

Government provision of information, along with other measures, plays an important role in reducing market failure.

Regulation

There are various forms of government **regulation** to correct market failure. In some cases direct controls are applied: for example, the Environmental Protection Act (1990) set minimum environmental standards for emissions from over 3,500 factories involved in chemical processes, waste incineration and oil refining. These firms are monitored by government pollution inspectors who have the power to impose fines and close down factories.

Regulation Government rules in markets to influence the behaviour of consumers and producers.

Advantages of regulations

- They are simple to understand: for example, legal restrictions on the age at which people can buy tobacco and alcohol.
- Limits can be imposed on the operation of firms to protect consumers: for example, a limit on the number of night air flights from Heathrow airport.
- It is possible to fine or close down companies that have abused the regulations: for example, by emitting dangerous levels of toxic waste.
- Fines act as a deterrent for both consumers and producers not to break the law. The revenue collected from fines could also be used to compensate victims.
- Regulations could require firms to restore and clean up the site after production: for example, in mining and quarrying operations.
- Regulations may help reduce the problem of asymmetric information: for example, restrictions on the sale of tobacco make it harder for young people to begin smoking, irrespective of whether they know how serious the consequences of smoking are.

Disadvantages of regulations

- Regulations can be expensive to monitor and enforce, as in the case of pollution levels imposed on firms. Administration costs can be high.
- Regulations may be set at the wrong level to correct market failure: for example, it is difficult to quantify and attach a monetary value to pollution emissions and so the social optimum position may not be reached.
- Regulations may increase the production costs of firms and make them less competitive in global markets, especially against firms in countries with few restrictions, such as China.

- Regulations may prevent the operation of the price mechanism, overruling it completely rather than working with it. In behavioural economics, regulations represent the use of 'shove' rather than 'nudge' policies.
- Unintended consequences may occur. For example, in regulatory capture, the regulator acts in the interest of the firms it is meant to regulate rather than the public it is meant to protect.

Government failure

Government failure occurs when government intervention leads to an inefficient allocation of resources and a net welfare loss. There are various types of government failure, such as the distortion of price signals, unintended consequences, excessive administration costs and information gaps. This links to the previous section, which covered the disadvantages of various government measures to correct market failure.

Before being too critical of government intervention, one should note that government failure is often less serious than the market failure it tries to solve. Without government intervention, the problems associated with market failure are likely to be far greater for both consumers and producers. For example, high taxes, health campaigns and regulations on tobacco and alcohol have helped reduce demand, leading to improved public health. However, it is useful to outline some types of government failure using relevant examples.

Distortion of price signals

Maximum and minimum price controls provide good examples of the **distortion of price signals** — how government intervention distorts the operation of the price mechanism and misallocates resources.

- *Maximum price controls* lead to an excess demand or shortage, as shown in Figure 30 for rental housing. Long-term implications include a reduction in both the quality and the quantity of rental housing available, possibly leading to an increase in the number of homeless.
- *Minimum price controls* lead to an excess supply or surplus, as shown in Figure 31 for agricultural products. Long-term implications include problems of disposing of food surpluses, which are perishable and expensive to store. Minimum price schemes may also require government expenditure on the surpluses, which has an opportunity cost.

Unintended consequences

Most types of government intervention have **unintended consequences**, as revealed by the following examples:

- *Indirect taxes* may lead to the development of illegal markets: for example, tobacco and alcohol smuggling. This leads to a growth in organised crime, counterfeit products and a loss of tax revenue for the government.
- *Subsidies* may lead to firms becoming dependent on them and inefficient in production. It may also be difficult to withdraw subsidies once they are in place: for example, grants to bus and rail companies.

Government failure
When government intervention leads to an inefficient allocation of resources and a net welfare loss.

Distortion of price signals The actions of government which distort the operation of the price mechanism and so misallocate resources.

Law of unintended consequences The actions of government, producers and consumers will always have effects that are unintended or unanticipated.

- *Maximum price* controls may lead to acute shortages of goods and services. The impact on private rental housing has already been discussed, but another example is a maximum wage for highly skilled workers: it could lead to a shortage of specialised workers in the banking sector that could undermine economic growth.
- *Minimum price controls* may lead to surpluses of goods and services. The impact on agricultural markets has already been discussed, but another example is a minimum wage for low-skilled workers: it could lead to unemployment as labour becomes too expensive for firms to employ.
- *Trade pollution permits* may not reduce carbon emissions so easily. For example, large polluting firms might find it easier and cheaper to buy spare permits on the market rather than invest in expensive equipment to reduce carbon emissions.
- *Regulations* may lead to regulatory capture. This is where the regulator acts in the interest of the firms, rather than of the consumers whom it is meant to protect.

Excessive administration costs

Government intervention in markets incurs **administration costs**, whether it concerns taxes, welfare benefits, subsidies, price controls, pollution permits or regulations. Sometimes the administration costs are so high as to put into question the cost effectiveness and validity of government intervention. These costs could arise in the formulation, monitoring or enforcement of government measures. Most areas of government intervention suffer from this and several examples are offered:

- Tax administration and collection can prove difficult and expensive for government: for example, tax changes in a budget may take a year to implement.
- Welfare benefits: in 2018 the government replaced various means-tested benefits (such as Jobseeker's Allowance and Housing Benefit) with the Universal Credit system in order to simplify the benefits system and increase financial incentives to work. However, according to the National Audit Office the new system is too cumbersome and beset with complaints and appeals by benefit recipients, giving little value for the money spent on it.
- Regulations require constant monitoring to ensure they are adhered to: for example, ensuring fishing boats do not exceed their fish catches or quotas.

Administration costs
The costs which arise in the formulation, monitoring and enforcing of government measures to correct market failure.

Information gaps

Information gaps can lead to government failure when the government lacks sufficient knowledge of the likely effects of its intervention in a particular market. This means the government could make non-rational decisions which lead to an inefficient allocation of resources and net welfare loss. We have previously shown how government intervention might fail by distorting market forces, causing unintended consequences and high administration costs. These are all linked to a lack of information in the first place concerning whether and how the government should intervene in a particular market. Several further examples are offered:

- The allocation of fish catches per boat (quotas) by EU governments appears to be set at too high a level, as the depletion of fish stocks continues. There is also the problem of fishing boats throwing back dead fish to keep within their quotas rather than risk large fines through landing their catch.

Information gaps
The government has insufficient information to make rational economic decisions.

- The EU governments failed to understand how the rest of world would react to the inclusion of air travel in the Emissions Trading Scheme. The EU has been forced to postpone the extension of the ETS due to threats of retaliatory taxes from other governments.
- A government setting a very high rate of income tax for top income earners might end up reducing the total tax take due to increased tax avoidance or evasion. This appeared to be the case in France (2013) where the government set a top rate of income tax of 75% for those workers earning more than 1 million euros per year.

Summary

- The government intervenes in different ways to correct market failure: for example, indirect taxation, subsidies, maximum and minimum prices, tradable pollution permits, provision of public goods, information and regulation.
- Indirect taxes and tradable pollution permits are used to limit production and internalise external costs to the market.
- Government subsidies are used to increase production and internalise external benefits to the market.
- Regulations are used to support the other measures and to set limits on activities that lead to market failure.
- Government failure may occur: this is where government intervention leads to an increase in inefficiency and a net welfare loss.
- Types of government failure include the distortion of price signals, unintended consequences, excessive administration costs and information gaps.
- Government failure is often less serious than the market failure it tries to solve.

Questions & Answers

Exam format

A-level Paper 1 — 'Markets and business behaviour' — comprises 35% of the weighting for the A-level examination. The paper comprises three sections: section A consists of five multiple-choice and short-answer questions; section B consists of one data-response question broken down into five sub-questions; section C consists of a choice of extended open-response questions — students select one from a choice of two.

The time allowed for the examination is 2 hours. There is a maximum of 100 marks: 25 marks are available in section A (the multiple-choice and short-answer questions), 50 marks in section B (the data-response question) and 25 marks in section C (the extended open-response question). This means around 25 minutes should be spent on section A, 60 minutes on section B and another 25 minutes on section C, leaving 10 minutes to check and amend your work.

Note: Paper 1 requires students to answer questions from Theme 1, 'Introduction to markets and market failure', and Theme 3, 'Business behaviour and the labour market'. Students are required to learn the models and concepts from both themes in preparation for the exam. You are recommended to obtain the accompanying student guide in this series, 'Business behaviour and the labour market'. This provides further guidance on the content and exam questions for Theme 3.

Section A

Multiple-choice and short-answer questions

This part of the book contains four sets of multiple-choice and short-answer questions. It is designed to be a key learning, revision and exam preparation resource. You should use these questions to reinforce your understanding of the specification subject matter and as practice for completing work under test conditions.

The multiple-choice and short-answer questions are similar in structure and style to the Paper 1 examination. In the examination, each question is often placed on a separate page in order to provide room for explanation, diagrams and calculations. There may be a lot more space than you need, so do not expect your answers to fill every page.

Each question is usually sub-divided into two or three parts which total 5 marks. Correct answers are given on pages 67–73, together with mark schemes indicating how the explanation marks would be awarded.

The nature of economics

Question 1

(a) Figure 1 shows a production possibility frontier for an economy.

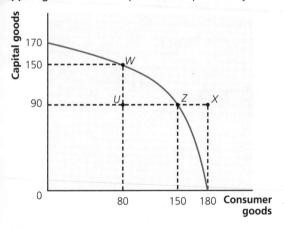

Figure 1

Which of the following is true? [1 mark]

A The opportunity cost of producing 80 consumer goods is 90 capital goods.

B There is an inefficient allocation of resources at position *U*.

C The opportunity cost of producing 180 consumer goods is 30 capital goods.

D Future economic growth is likely to be higher at position *Z* than *W*.

(b) With reference to the diagram, explain how the production possibility frontier can illustrate opportunity cost. [2 marks]

(c) Explain one factor that could increase a country's rate of economic growth — as shown by an outward shift of the production possibility frontier. [2 marks]

Question 2

(a) Table 1 shows the functions of money along with its key benefits. Which function of money is correctly linked to its key benefit? [1 mark]

Table 1

Option	Function	Key benefit
A	Medium of exchange	Eliminates the need for barter
B	Measure of value	Convenient way of holding wealth
C	Store of value	Enables borrowing and lending to take place
D	Method of deferred payment	Enables comparison of the relative values of products

(b) In 2018 Venezuela's inflation rate reached 500,000%. Explain why it is important for money to be scarce. [2 marks]

(c) Statement 1: Venezuela has the world's highest proven oil reserves, which exceed 300 billion barrels.

Statement 2: It is unfair that the Venezuelan government has reduced domestic fuel subsidies for its citizens.

With reference to the statements above, distinguish between positive and normative economics. [2 marks]

Question 3

(a) Three people work in a small bakery, each dividing their time equally between making three types of cake. Table 2 shows how many cakes are made by each worker per day. [1 mark]

Table 2

	Chocolate éclair Daily quantity	Custard tart Daily quantity	Carrot cake Daily quantity
Pauline	40	80	20
Sue	20	40	80
Ruth	80	20	40
Total output	140	140	140

If division of labour is introduced and each worker concentrates on making the cake she is most productive at, then the combined total daily output will increase by:

A   60

B   100

C   160

D   300

(b) Outline two likely reasons why the bakery workers are able to produce more cakes through the division of labour. [2 marks]

(c) Explain one possible disadvantage of the division of labour for a bakery. [2 marks]

Question 4

(a) Which of the following statements best describes how a free market economy differs from a mixed economy? [1 mark]

    A Business is organised to produce necessities rather than luxuries.

    B Essential services such as healthcare and education are provided free to all and funded from taxation.

    C The vast majority of resources are allocated by the price mechanism.

    D Most resources are owned and controlled by the government.

(b) Outline two benefits created by competition in a free market economy. [2 marks]

(c) With reference to Table 3, explain one advantage of healthcare provision in a command economy (such as Cuba), compared to that of a market-based economy (such as the USA). [2 marks]

Table 3

	Cuba	USA
Income per capita in 2017 ($US)	$5,900	$53,700
Infant mortality rate in 2017 (number of deaths before the age of 1 year per thousand)	4.1	5.7

Question 5

(a) Table 4 shows UK electricity generation from renewable sources between 2013 and 2017. [1 mark]

Table 4 UK electricity output from renewable sources (Gigawatt hours)

Year	Output of electricity (GWh)	Index numbers of electricity output (base year 2014)
2013	52,213	
2014	64,522	100.0
2015	83,364	129.3
2016	83,127	128.9
2017	99,330	

Source: Department for Business, Energy and Industrial Strategy, 2018

The table shows that electricity output from renewable sources increased:

    A every year

    B at the fastest rate between 2013 and 2014

    C by 16.32% between 2016 and 2017

    D at the fastest rate between 2016 and 2017

(b) Using the table, calculate the index numbers for 2013 and 2017. [2 marks]

(c) Explain one likely reason for the trend in UK electricity generation from renewable sources. [2 marks]

How markets work

Question 1

Table 1 shows the market for luxury chocolates. The original equilibrium price is £18 per box.

Table 1

Price per box (£)	Quantity demanded per month	Quantity supplied per month	New quantity demanded per month	New quantity supplied per month
16	3,400	3,000		
17	3,300	3,100		
18	3,200	3,200		
19	3,100	3,300		
20	3,000	3,400		

As a result of a rise in production costs, the supply of luxury chocolates decreases by 200 at every price level. At the same time, a fall in the price of fudge causes the demand for luxury chocolates to decrease by 400 at every price level.

(a) Calculate the new equilibrium price and quantity of luxury chocolates following a rise in production costs and a fall in the price of fudge. Use the last two columns for your workings. [2 marks]

(b) Calculate the change in monthly total revenue for producers of luxury chocolates. [2 marks]

(c) The relationship between chocolate and fudge is that they are: [1 mark]

    A   substitutes with a negative cross elasticity of demand

    B   complements with a positive cross elasticity of demand

    C   substitutes with a positive cross elasticity of demand

    D   complements with a negative cross elasticity of demand

Question 2

Table 2 shows a utility schedule for an individual consuming mini-chocolate cakes in one evening.

Table 2

Mini cakes consumed	Total utility (units)	Marginal utility (units)
0	0	
1	8	
2	18	
3	30	
4	40	
5	48	
6	54	
7	56	
8	54	

(a) Calculate the marginal utility for each mini-chocolate cake consumed over one evening. Use the last column in the table to show your workings. [2 marks]

(b) Diminishing marginal utility first occurs on consumption of the: [1 mark]
   A   first mini-cake
   B   third mini-cake
   C   fourth mini-cake
   D   eighth mini-cake

(c) Explain the relevance of 'diminishing marginal utility' to the downward-sloping demand curve. [2 marks]

Question 3

(a) Research has estimated the price elasticity of demand for fair trade coffee at −0.5. Other things remaining equal, a 15% increase in price will cause the percentage quantity demand for fair trade coffee to fall by: [1 mark]
   A   0.2
   B   0.75
   C   2.0
   D   7.5

(b) Explain the likely effect of the increase in price on total revenue for fair trade coffee producers. Use a diagram in your answer. [2 marks]

(c) Explain one factor which is likely to affect the price elasticity of demand for fair trade coffee. [2 marks]

Question 4

Between 2015 and 2016, average UK real household disposable income rose from £26,300 to £26,700. Over the same period, the total miles of car vehicle travel also increased from 248 billion to 253 billion miles.

(a) Ceteris paribus, calculate the income elasticity of demand for car vehicle travel. [1 mark]

(b) The demand for car vehicle travel is: [1 mark]
   A   a normal good and income elastic
   B   an inferior good and income inelastic
   C   a normal good and income inelastic
   D   an inferior good and income elastic

(c) With reference to the concept of cross elasticity of demand, explain two possible alternative reasons for the increase in demand for car vehicle travel. [3 marks]

Question 5

Table 3 shows the monthly demand and supply schedules for a luxury range of caviar. (You may use the blank column for your explanation.)

Table 3

Price per box (£)	Quantity demanded (boxes)	Quantity supplied (boxes)	New quantity supplied (boxes)
60	220	280	
50	230	270	
40	240	260	
30	250	250	
20	260	240	
10	270	230	

(a) If the government decides to introduce an indirect tax of £20 per box of caviar, what is the new equilibrium price and quantity? [1 mark]

(b) (i) The total tax revenue collected by the government each month is: [1 mark]
   A   £1,250
   B   £2,400
   C   £4,800
   D   £5,000
   (ii) Calculate the percentage share of the tax paid by consumers. [1 mark]

(c) Explain one likely reason for the government imposing a tax on caviar. [2 marks]

Market failure

Question 1

(a) All of the following are examples of market failure except: [1 mark]
   A   asymmetric information between buyers and sellers in the second-hand car market
   B   under-provision of street lighting in a free market economy
   C   air pollution and road congestion from driving motor vehicles
   D   government minimum price controls in agriculture that lead to an excess supply of food

(b) Distinguish between a private good and a public good. [1 mark]

(c) Explain why a coastal flood defence scheme is unlikely to be provided in a free market economy. [3 marks]

Question 2

(a) Negative externalities exist in a market when: [1 mark]
   A   production costs are internalised by the price mechanism
   B   social costs exceed the private costs in production
   C   social costs are less than the private costs in production
   D   social costs equal the private costs in production

(b) Figure 1 shows the market for fracked gas. Assuming no government intervention, explain why market failure is likely to occur. Refer to the concept of welfare loss in your answer. [4 marks]

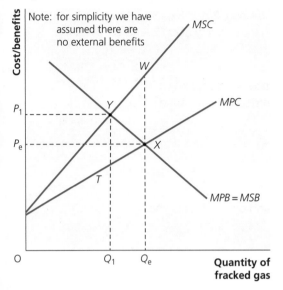

Figure 1

Question 3

(a) Figure 2 shows the market for rail travel. Assume there are no external costs and no government intervention. The current equilibrium quantity is Q_e and the equilibrium price is P_e. By increasing the quantity of rail journeys it is possible to: [1 mark]

  A achieve a welfare gain of MTX
  B eliminate an excess supply of XV
  C achieve a welfare gain of TXR
  D eliminate government failure

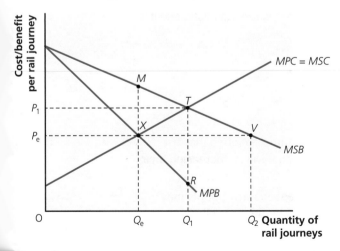

Figure 2

(b) Annotate the diagram to show how a government subsidy to rail operating firms could lead to the socially optimum level of output in the market. [2 marks]

(c) The number of rail passenger journeys in Britain increased from 387 million in Quarter 1 of 2012 to 428 million in Quarter 1 of 2018 (Office of Rail and Road, 2019). Explain one external benefit that might arise from such an increase in the quantity of rail journeys. [2 marks]

Question 4

(a) Over one-quarter of British holiday makers fail to take out travel insurance when taking foreign holidays. A likely reason for the underconsumption of insurance in the holiday travel market is that: [1 mark]

A external benefits exist

B holiday insurance is non-excludable

C an information gap exists

D holiday insurance is non-rivalrous in consumption

(b) Table 1 shows alcohol-related hospital admissions in England over selected years.

Table 1

Year	Number of alcohol-related hospital admissions
2006	681,380
2011	992,400
2016	1,119,020

Source: National Statistics, 2017

   (i) Calculate the percentage increase in the number of alcohol-related hospital admissions between 2006 and 2016. [1 mark]

   (ii) Explain one possible cause of the trend shown. [2 marks]

(c) Outline how imperfect market information might lead to excess consumption of alcohol. [1 mark]

Question 5

(a) A private pension fund forecasts a high rate of return on its retirement products, which convinces thousands of people to purchase them. However, further research by the pension fund reveals that such a forecast is too optimistic and it fails to inform its customers for fear of losing sales.

This is an example of: [1 mark]

A asymmetric information

B moral hazard

C rationing sales

D habitual behaviour

(b) In 2017 a survey conducted by the Financial Conduct Authority found that 15 million adults in the UK had little or no private pension savings, increasing their likelihood of living in poverty during old age.

With reference to market failure, outline two possible reasons why people may not make sufficient contributions to a private pension scheme during their working lives. [2 marks]

(c) Table 2 shows the projected life expectancy for people once they have reached the age of 65 years in the UK between 2011 and 2050. Explain the significance of these data for private pension contributions. [2 marks]

Table 2 Life expectancy for people on reaching the age of 65 in the year shown

Year	2011	2015	2020	2030	2040	2050
Women (years)	23.8	24.3	24.9	26.0	27.1	28.2
Men (years)	21.1	21.7	22.2	23.4	24.6	25.8

Source: Pensions Policy Institute, 2019

Government intervention

Question 1

(a) Greenhouse gas emissions are projected to fall by 21% in the industries covered by the EU Emissions Trading System between 2005 and 2020. The most likely reason for this reduction in pollution is the: [1 mark]

    A   increase in cost of applying clean technology to production

    B   decrease in subsidies for renewable energy firms

    C   increase in market price of pollution permits

    D   difficulty in monitoring carbon emissions from firms

(b) A chemical company generates 15,000 tons of carbon pollution over the year, exceeding its free allocation of 8,000 tons of carbon pollution permits, granted under the European Emissions Trading System. The company purchases the additional carbon permits in the market at a price of 18 euros per ton. Calculate the total cost to the firm of the carbon pollution permits. [2 marks]

(c) Explain one reason why EU tradable pollution permits may be ineffective in reducing global carbon emissions. [2 marks]

Question 2

(a) A government imposes a maximum price on medicinal drugs that is set below the free market price. Explain the likely effects on the market for medicinal drugs. Use a supply and demand diagram in your answer. [4 marks]

(b) A government imposes a maximum price on fresh milk that is set above the free market price. The most likely effect of this maximum price is that: [1 mark]

    A   the quantity of milk demanded will fall

    B   new dairy farmers will join the market to increase the quantity supplied

    C   there will be an excess supply of milk

    D   there is no effect on the market price or quantity of milk

Question 3

(a) A government imposes a minimum price on alcohol of 75p per unit compared to the free market price of 50p per unit. Explain the likely effects on the market for alcohol. Use a supply and demand diagram in your answer. [4 marks]

(b) The most likely reason for a government imposing a minimum price for alcohol is to: [1 mark]

    A   decrease market price

    B   increase quantity supplied

    C   decrease market failure

    D   increase producer surplus

Question 4

(a) The tax on a packet of cigarettes comprises 90% of its price. Calculate the tax paid (in pounds and pence) on a packet of cigarettes priced at £12.50. [1 mark]

(b) Explain one likely unintended consequence of the high tax on cigarettes. [2 marks]

(c) Table 1 shows the percentage of adults in Britain who smoke (2002–17).

Table 1 Adult smoking rates in Britain, 2002–17

Year	2002	2006	2010	2014	2017
Men (%)	27	23	21	20	17
Women (%)	25	21	20	17	13

Source: Action on Smoking and Health

Using the table and your own knowledge, explain one government regulatory measure which may have helped cause the trend shown. [2 marks]

Question 5

(a) Figure 1 shows the impact of a government unit subsidy placed on the production of solar panels. Which of the following is correct? [1 mark]

   A   Consumer surplus increases by P_1P_2FX.
   B   The total subsidy area is OP_2FQ_2.
   C   Producer surplus increases by P_1XY.
   D   The solar panel price falls by the same amount as the unit subsidy.

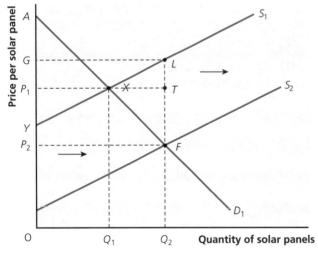

Figure 1

(b) The total US federal government subsidy for the production of electricity from solar power was $4,393 million in 2015. Total output of electricity from solar power was 19 million megawatts (Institute for Energy Research, 2015). Calculate the subsidy per megawatt of electricity produced from solar power. [1 mark]

(c) In 2019 the UK government scrapped subsidies for solar power. Explain why government subsidies may lead to 'government failure' in a market. [3 marks]

Answers to multiple-choice and short-answer questions

The nature of economics

Question 1

(a) Correct answer **B**, as there are unemployed resources — so allocatively inefficient. [1 mark]

(b) Opportunity costs can be illustrated on a production possibility frontier by moving along it. For example, a movement from *W* to *Z* involves an increase in output of consumer goods by 70 units and a decrease in output of capital goods by 60 units/this is because some resources have to be reallocated from capital goods production to consumer goods production. [1 + 1 marks]

(c) Economic growth could be increased by allocating more resources to capital goods and relatively less to consumer goods production/this leads to more factories and machinery and improved technology, which could then be used to increase the production of consumer goods. [1 + 1 marks]

Question 2

(a) Correct answer **A**, since as a medium of exchange, money eliminates the requirement for a double coincidence of wants to enable a market transaction to take place. [1 mark]

(b) Money needs to be scarce so that it will be generally acceptable in the payment for goods and services/otherwise, its value would fall so rapidly that it would cease to be used for buying goods and services as in the case of Venezuela. Alternative forms of money are then used: for example, the US dollar. [1 + 1 marks]

(c) Statement 1 is an example of positive economics, which refers to the use of facts that can be tested as true or false. In this example, it is true that Venezuela has the world's largest known oil reserves as found by geologists testing for deposits. Statement 2 is an example of normative economics, which refers to the use of value judgements (unfair) which cannot be falsified. Some people will agree but others will disagree. [1 + 1 marks]

Question 3

(a) Correct answer **D**, as Pauline would specialise in custard tarts, producing 240. Sue would specialise in carrot cakes (240) and Ruth in chocolate éclairs (240). The daily total is 720, which is 300 more than the original total of 420. [1 mark]

(b) Reasons for an increase in total output include: repetition leads to an increase in skill and productivity/less time is required moving from one task to another task. [1 + 1 marks]

(c) One disadvantage is that boredom might set in from a worker carrying out the same monotonous task/so product quality might fall or there could be a high rate of staff absenteeism. [1 + 1 marks]

Question 4

(a) Correct answer **C**, as free market economies are characterised by minimal government intervention, so the price mechanism allocates resources. [1 mark]

(b) Benefits due to competition in a free market economy include: an increase in efficiency as firms have an incentive to keep unit costs of production down, leading to lower prices/improved product quality as consumers have increased choice/greater investment as entrepreneurs strive to outcompete rivals to gain higher profits. [1 + 1 marks]

(c) Healthcare in a command economy is provided free of charge to all at the point of consumption — unlike in market-based economies/consequently, Cuba has a lower infant mortality rate (4.1) than the USA (5.7), despite having a much lower average income per head. [1 + 1 marks]

Question 5

(a) Correct answer **B**, as electricity output from renewable sources increased by 23.58%. [1 mark]

(b) 2013 = 81.0 (accept 80.9); 2017 = 154.0 (accept 153.9). [1 + 1 marks]

(c) Government subsidies to renewable energy electricity production/which helped to reduce production costs and so make it more competitive in comparison with fossil fuel energy. (Accept government regulations and taxation of non-renewable energy sources/which make them less competitive). [1 + 1 marks]

How markets work

Question 1

(a) New equilibrium price is £17 and quantity is 2,900. [1 + 1 marks]

Price per box (£)	Quantity demanded per month	Quantity supplied per month	New quantity demanded per month	New quantity supplied per month
16	3,400	3,000	3,000	2,800
17	3,300	3,100	2,900	2,900
18	3,200	3,200	2,800	3,000
19	3,100	3,300	2,700	3,100
20	3,000	3,400	2,600	3,200

(b) Original total revenue is £18 × 3,200 = £57,600.

New total revenue is £17 × 2,900 = £49,300.

The change is –£8,300. [2 marks]

(c) Correct answer **C**. [1 mark]

Question 2

(a)

Mini cakes consumed	Total utility (units)	Marginal utility (units)
0	0	–
1	8	8
2	18	10
3	30	12
4	40	10
5	48	8
6	54	6
7	56	2
8	54	–2

[2 marks for all correct answers in final column; 1 mark for between two and five correct answers]

(b) Correct answer **C**, as marginal utility falls to 10 units. [1 mark]

(c) As one consumes additional units of a good, marginal utility will eventually diminish (as with the fourth mini-cake)/this suggests that an individual will only be prepared to buy more of a good as its price falls, since marginal utility is also falling. [1 + 1 marks]

Question 3

(a) Correct answer **D**, as $-7.5 \div 15 = -0.5$. [1 mark]

(b) Total revenue is likely to increase for fair trade coffee producers since demand is price inelastic/diagram shows how the rise in price leads to total revenue increasing from OP_eXQ_e to OP_1YQ_1. [1 + 1 marks]

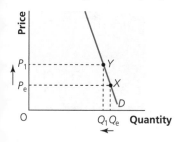

(c) The availability and closeness of substitutes such as non-fair traded coffee or tea/an increase in the availability and quality of these substitutes is likely to make fair trade coffee more price elastic in demand. [1 + 1 marks]

Question 4

(a) Income elasticity of demand for car vehicle travel is 1.33; $(2.01\% \div 1.52\% = 1.33)$. [1 mark]

(b) Correct answer **A**, as a positive answer (normal good) and elastic (above 1.0). [1 mark]

(c) Accept various causes: fall in price of complementary goods such as fuel/ complementary goods have a negative cross elasticity of demand [1 + 1 marks]; a rise in price of substitute goods such as bus and rail travel/substitutes have a positive cross elasticity of demand [1 + 1 marks]. Note a maximum of 3 marks available here.

Question 5

(a) New equilibrium price is £40 and quantity is 240. [1 mark]

Price per box (£)	Quantity demanded (boxes)	Quantity supplied (boxes)	New quantity supplied (boxes)
60	220	280	260
50	230	270	250
40	240	260	240
30	250	250	230
20	260	240	
10	270	230	

(b) (i) Correct answer **C**, as the total tax revenue collected per month is
£20 × 240 = £4,800. [1 mark]

    (ii) Consumers pay 50% of the tax (shown by the rise in market price of
£10 × 240 = £2,400). [1 mark]

(c) Caviar is a sustainable resource if carefully managed/so reduce consumption and
production in order to preserve fish stocks for future generations. Also accept idea
of raising tax revenue and equity reasons with some development. [1 + 1 marks]

Market failure

Question 1

(a) Correct answer **D**, as this is an example of government failure, preventing
agricultural markets from reaching equilibrium. [1 mark]

(b) A private good has characteristics of rivalry and excludability in consumption
whereas a public good has characteristics of non-rivalry and non-excludability. [1 mark]

(c) A coastal flood defence scheme is unlikely to be provided in a free market
economy, since it is a public good characterised by non-rivalry and non-
excludability in consumption/this leads to a free-rider problem where people can
consume a good for free once it has been provided/so no incentive for firms to
provide it as they cannot make a profit. [1 + 1 + 1 marks]

Question 2

(a) Correct answer **B**, as social cost is the sum of external costs and private costs. [1 mark]

(b) Market failure is likely to occur since the price mechanism ignores external costs
from fracking/these include air, water and visual pollution which reduce nearby
property prices/the free market output of OQ_e exceeds the social optimum output
of OQ_1/so the social cost of the output slice (Q_eQ_1YW) exceeds the social benefit
(Q_eQ_1TX)/this causes a welfare loss of WXY. [1 + 1 + 1 + 1 marks]

Question 3

(a) Correct answer **A**, as social benefit (MTQ_1Q_e) exceeds social cost (XTQ_1Q_e) for
output slice Q_eQ_1. [1 mark]

(b) Shift the $MPC=MSC$ curve to the right to $MPC_1=MSC_1$ where social optimum
output OQ_1 is reached/identify subsidy area (such as P_1TRP_0). [1 + 1 marks]

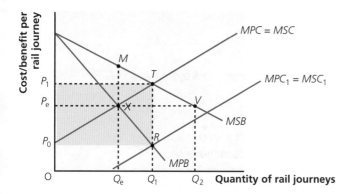

(c) External benefits from rail travel include less road congestion and air pollution as motorists leave their cars at home and undertake more rail journeys/this could mean faster motor vehicle journey times which reduce transport costs and increase efficiency for firms, or a reduction in respiratory illnesses and so less pressure on state healthcare services.   [1 + 1 marks]

Question 4

(a) Correct answer **C**, as many holiday makers do not realise the high costs of foreign healthcare if they have an accident or become ill overseas.   [1 mark]

(b) (i) $\dfrac{1{,}119{,}200 - 681{,}380}{681{,}380} \times 100 = 64.25\%$ [1 mark]

   (ii) Identification of one reason with development, e.g. incomes have risen at a faster rate than the price of alcohol/so it is more affordable to consume.   [1 + 1 marks]

(c) Lack of market knowledge about the strength of alcohol in drinks or the size of alcoholic drinks, so consumers may end up drinking far more than intended.   [1 mark]

Question 5

(a) Correct answer **A**, as the producer (pension company) has more market knowledge than consumers about the forecast returns, leading to consumers making misinformed choices.   [1 mark]

(b) Reasons include: people may not earn sufficient income to afford to contribute to a pension scheme/possibility of being unemployed for some of the working-age period/lack of consumer knowledge about pension contributions/self-employed are not automatically enrolled in a private pension scheme/pension age is a long way off for most workers, so they may delay starting pension contributions/preference for more income in short term compared to extra income in retirement.   [1 + 1 marks]

(c) The data indicate that people should increase their pension contributions as these funds will have to last for longer due to increased life expectancy on reaching the age of 65/reference to data, e.g. women are projected to live for an extra 4.4 years and men 4.7 years/women live longer than men and so perhaps need to make larger contributions to private pensions.   [1 + 1 marks]

Government intervention

Question 1

(a) Correct answer **C**, as the increase in price of pollution permits gives firms a greater incentive to switch to cleaner energy sources. [1 mark]

(b) Answer is $7{,}000 \times 18$ euros $= 126{,}000$ euros. [2 marks]

(c) Reasons include: most other countries in the world are not part of a tradable pollution permits scheme/difficulty in monitoring and enforcing restrictions on pollution emissions/air travel industry remains outside of the Emissions Trading Scheme [1 mark]. Development of a reason, e.g. in such circumstances the price mechanism is unable to operate to limit carbon emissions [1 mark]. [1 + 1 marks]

Question 2

(a) A maximum price of P_1 will lead to an excess demand or shortage of medicinal drugs/demand extends to Q_2 and supply contracts to Q_1/unintended consequences include a hidden market being created for medicinal drugs where prices exceed the legal maximum [up to 1 + 1 marks]. Relevant diagram identifying the maximum price/excess demand of Q_1Q_2 [up to 1 + 1 marks]. [4 marks]

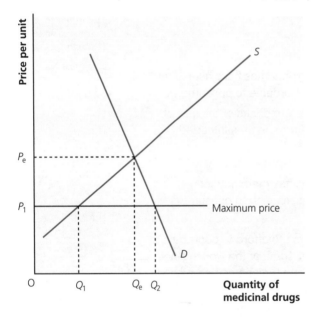

(b) Correct answer **D**, as a maximum price is just a ceiling price. The market price of milk can be in equilibrium at any price below the maximum price. [1 mark]

Question 3

(a) A minimum price of 75p per unit will lead to an excess supply or surplus of alcohol/demand contracts to Q_1 and supply extends to Q_2/unintended consequences include illegal selling of alcohol below the minimum price [up to 1 + 1 marks]. Relevant diagram identifying the minimum price/excess supply of Q_1Q_2 [up to 1 + 1 marks]. [4 marks]

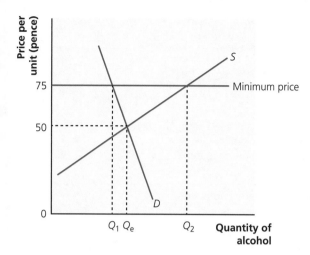

(b) Correct option **C**, as market failure occurs because the price mechanism ignores external costs associated with alcohol consumption, e.g. violent crime. [1 mark]

Question 4

(a) Correct answer: £11.25 (90 × £12.50 ÷ 100). [1 mark]

(b) A hidden market may develop involving tobacco smuggling/this may reduce tax revenue for the government/increases cost of monitoring tobacco sales and enforcing the law. [1 + 1 marks]

(c) The table shows that adult smoking rates fell between 2002 and 2017, from 27 to 17 percentage points for men and from 25 to 13 percentage points for women [1 mark]. A regulatory measure may include the legislation banning smoking in enclosed places such as pubs and restaurants, making smoking less socially acceptable [1 mark]. [2 marks]

Question 5

(a) Correct answer **A**, as consumer surplus increases from AXP_1 to AFP_2. [1 mark]

(b) $4,393 million ÷ 19 million megawatts = $231.2 per megawatt. [1 mark]

(c) Definition of government failure/government subsidies may cause firms to become dependent on them and so lead to inefficiency in production/waste of taxpayers' money/opportunity cost of subsidy. [1 + 1 + 1 marks]

■Section B

Data-response questions

Structure of the questions

The data-response questions comprise five compulsory sub-questions labelled (a) to (e), which total 50 marks. Question 1 is on the UK bottled water market and question 2 focuses on the UK housing market.

A 'levels'-based approach is used to mark the data-response and the extended open-response questions (section C). This enables a variety of different approaches in student answers to be valid rather than solely requiring specific points that are stated on the mark scheme. It means the examiner makes an initial assessment of the quality of an answer and places it at a level ranging from 1 to 4. The examiner's judgement is then refined to award a more precise mark within that level. It is recommended that you refer to the levels descriptors provided in the sample assessment materials for Economics produced by Edexcel at:

https://tinyurl.com/y2o8h38b

In addition, a levels-based mark scheme is often broken down into two further parts: the first focuses on 'knowledge, application and analysis' marks and the second relates to 'evaluation'. Evaluation questions include the command words *examine, evaluate, assess, discuss* and *to what extent*. Any of these instructions indicate that you should demonstrate some critical understanding of the issues being discussed.

Each sub-question here is followed by some general guidance on how the question should be approached. You are advised to attempt the questions before you read the sample student answers supplied. Student answers are followed by detailed comments which show you what is being rewarded and how the answer might have been improved.

Question 1 The UK bottled water market

Table 1 UK bottled water market and real income per head

Year	Consumption (million litres)	Consumption per head (litres)	Sales revenue (£ million)	Real household disposable income per head (£)
2011	1,879	29.7	1,099	17,991
2012	1,896	29.8	1,139	18,257
2013	2,022	31.6	1,251	18,119
2014	2,207	34.2	1,368	18,254
2015	2,407	37.0	1,485	18,770
2016	2,637	40.3	1,602	18,917

Sources: British Soft Drinks Association, Annual Report, 2017; Office for National Statistics

Table 2 UK fizzy soft drinks*

Year	Consumption fizzy drinks (million litres)	Consumption fizzy drinks per head (litres)
2011	5,443	86.0
2012	5,360	84.1
2013	5,350	83.5
2014	5,240	81.1
2015	5,201	79.9
2016	5,192	79.2

* Fizzy soft drinks refer to colas, lemonade, tonics and other sparkling fruit-flavoured drinks.

Source: British Soft Drinks Association, Annual Report, 2017

Extract A Bottled water sales and consumer behaviour

Bottled water has become the world's best-selling soft drink. In the UK alone over 2.6 billion litres of it was drunk in 2016. Its growth in consumption is linked to convenience, quality and taste. Yet tap water can be obtained almost for free. Bottled water is between 500 and 2,000 times more expensive than tap water. It may also be less safe to drink than tap water due to micro plastic contamination and the chemicals which gradually build up in bottles. By contrast, tap water is regulated by the Drinking Water Inspectorate which takes regular samples, where 99.7% pass strict standards. Although tiny amounts of chlorine are added to tap water affecting its taste, this is required to destroy harmful bacteria.

Extract B Environmental costs of bottled water

Bottled water is harmful to the environment. It takes 3 litres of water to produce 1 litre of bottled water. The production of bottled water leaves a large carbon footprint, creating over 160 grams of carbon dioxide per litre — equivalent to driving a petrol-engine car for 1 kilometre. Recycling rates are also poor; in the UK some 35 million plastic bottles are consumed everyday — but 16 million of them are not recycled; much of this waste ends up in landfill sites or, worse still, in the oceans, destroying marine life. The average plastic water bottle takes 400 years to decompose.

However, over recent years UK bottle manufacturers have switched to using recyclable plastic materials and new designs which are 30% lighter, using less plastic. Yet most plastic bottles can only be recycled twice before they become unusable anyway.

Although bottled water is already subject to a 20% value added tax, there have been calls for imposing an additional specific tax in order to reduce consumption and help protect the environment. Proponents have pointed out how the 5p tax on plastic carrier bags introduced in 2015 led to an 85% reduction in demand. Further options include regulations: for example, implementing a bottle deposit scheme and compelling manufacturers to use substitute materials such as glass and aluminium.

(a) With reference to Table 1, explain the effect on the total sales revenue of bottled water companies, following an increase in demand for bottled water between 2011 and 2016. Use a demand and supply diagram in your answer. [5 marks]

> This is the only question in the data response with no evaluation marks. All the marks are for knowledge, application and analysis. Ensure a demand and supply diagram is provided or your marks will be capped, usually at a maximum of 3 out of 5 marks. Make explicit use of the bottled water data in Table 1 or, again, risk being capped. Use of the data will count towards the quantitative aspects of the assessment.

(b) With reference to Tables 1 and 2, examine two likely reasons for the increase in consumption per head of bottled water. [8 marks]

> Offer two possible causes of the increase in consumption per head of bottled water, making explicit use of the data in both Tables 1 and 2. Usually 2 knowledge marks are available for identifying two causes from the data. Try and offer some development of the data to gain 2 application marks: for example, by calculating the increase in consumption of bottled water and the decrease in consumption of substitutes such as fizzy drinks. By developing the reasoning for the increase in demand for bottled water, 2 analysis marks can be achieved. There are also 2 marks available for an evaluative comment here, so make sure one is offered.

(c) With reference to Extract A and your own knowledge, discuss whether the increase in consumption of bottled water represents rational consumer behaviour. [10 marks]

> This question invites you to consider both views, one being that consumers are behaving rationally, the other that they are not. Typically, the best answered view is awarded up to 6 knowledge, application and analysis marks; the alternative view is then awarded up to 4 evaluation marks. This flexibility in marking enables candidates to achieve the highest mark possible, given the quality of their answer.

(d) With reference to Extract B and your own knowledge, evaluate the possible costs of an increase in production and consumption of bottled water. Use an external cost diagram in your answer. [12 marks]

> It is useful to consider both the private and external costs to producers and consumers. Also ensure a suitable external cost diagram is offered or your marks will be capped, usually to a Level 2 answer (maximum of 5 out of 8 knowledge, application and analysis marks). There are also 4 evaluation marks available and this usually requires one (very well-developed) or two comments. Evaluation may come in the form of considering the possible benefits from the growth in the bottled water market.

(e) Discuss whether the introduction of a specific tax is likely to be more effective than regulations in reducing external costs from the bottled water market. [15 marks]

> Make sure you consider the merits of both specific taxation and regulations on bottled water in order to avoid being capped (usually to a Level 2 answer — a maximum of 6 out of 9 knowledge, application and analysis marks). There are 6 evaluation marks available and this usually requires two comments.

Student answer

(a) The diagram shows an increase in demand for bottled water from D_1 to D_2, raising both price and quantity from P_1 to P_2 and Q_1 to Q_2. Total revenue increases from OP_1XQ_1 to OP_2YQ_2. [a]

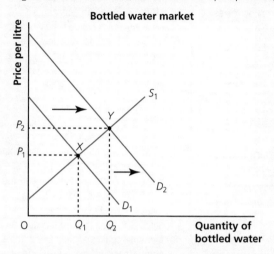

Bottled water market

(b) Table 1 shows that consumption per head of bottled water has increased from 29.7 litres in 2011 to 40.3 litres in 2016. This is a growth of more than 35%. One likely reason for this is due to a decrease in demand for substitute goods such as fizzy drinks (consumption per head has fallen by 7.9%) shown in Table 2. The substitutes may have increased in price, leading to an increase in demand for bottled water, reflecting a positive cross elasticity of demand relationship between them. It could also be due to a change in tastes and fashion, where many consumers have become more health conscious and so have switched from sugary fizzy drinks to bottled water. [b]

A second likely reason for the increase in demand for bottled water is due to a rise in real household disposable income per head as shown in Table 1. Between 2011 and 2016 real income per head increased by £926 or 5.1%, making it more affordable to buy bottled water. This also suggests that bottled water is a normal good with a positive income elasticity of demand. [c]

(c) Rational consumer behaviour assumes individuals allocate their income so that they maximise their total utility when spending on goods and services. [d] However, the rapid growth in consumption of bottled water suggests that consumers are not acting rationally since it is between 500 and 2,000 times more expensive than readily available tap water. There is an opportunity cost to buying bottled water as people could spend this money on other goods and services instead; they just

(a) [a] An accurate diagram is shown depicting an increase in demand (1 application mark), and the original and new areas of total revenue (1 knowledge and 1 analysis mark). However, no direct reference is made to Table 1 as required. Further application and analysis marks could be obtained by using the data: for example, the total sales revenue for bottled water companies increased by 46% from £1,099 million in 2011 to £1,602 million in 2016. **3/5 marks awarded.**

(b) [b] The student explicitly uses the data in Tables 1 and 2 to explain two likely causes of the increase in demand for bottled water (1 + 1 knowledge marks). The first cause relates to the fall in consumption of substitute goods such as fizzy drinks, and some relevant analysis is offered using cross elasticity of demand (1 application and 1 analysis mark). [c] The second cause is linked to the rise in real household disposable income, and further analysis is offered using income elasticity of demand (1 application and 1 analysis mark). Manipulation of the data includes calculating the percentage increase in sales of bottled water and the decrease in sales of fizzy drinks.

Although all the available knowledge, application and analysis marks have been achieved, the student slips up by not offering an evaluative comment and so can only gain a maximum of 6 out of 8 marks. One evaluation technique which could be used here is to raise the possibility of other factors causing the trend in bottled water consumption: for example, advertising campaigns or higher taxes on substitute goods. This makes it difficult to decide the relative importance of different factors. **6/8 marks awarded.**

have to replace bottled water with tap water, the latter being widely available in homes. e

Government regulations also mean the quality of tap water is high — it contains traces of chlorine which kills most harmful bacteria. Extract A mentions that 99.7% of water samples pass the strict standards set. By contrast, bottled water appears to have less stringent regulations and may suffer from micro plastic contamination which could harm consumers. On this basis, it appears consumers of bottled water are not behaving rationally since it may be of poorer quality than tap water. f

(d) External costs are negative third-party effects ignored by the market transaction. There are external costs in both the production and consumption of bottled water. These include a large carbon footprint which the extract mentions is over 160 grams of CO_2 per litre bottle. Chemical processes involved in making the plastic emit gases which add to global warming. Some 35 million plastic bottles are used every day in the UK but 16 million are not recycled. This has led to an enormous amount of plastic waste being deposited in landfill sites and in the oceans, damaging marine life. The increase in production and consumption of bottled water can only make things much worse. g

External costs of bottled water

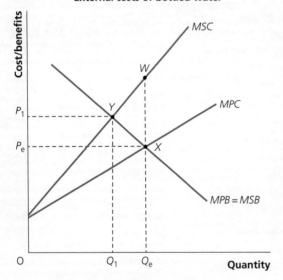

However, it should also be recognised that there are many benefits from the growth in the bottled water industry. Jobs have been created and incomes increased in the sector. It also generates more profits for bottled water companies and dividends for shareholders. There are positive multiplier effects throughout the supply chain, benefiting other industries,

(c) d The student outlines the meaning of rational consumer behaviour and then uses the information in Extract A to explain two reasons why the trend for consuming more bottled water is irrational. e The first concerns its high price and the second f questions its quality. Two points, well developed, are sufficient to award the maximum knowledge (2), application (2) and analysis (2) marks available.

As with the previous answer, the student fails to offer any evaluation and so can only achieve 6 out of 10 marks. A useful evaluation technique is to investigate the other side of the argument — that consumer behaviour is rational, for example, as long as the marginal benefit gained exceeds or equals the price paid for the last unit. More use could also be made of the phrase 'convenience, quality and taste' of bottled water in Extract A. Tap water is not always available to people in their busy lives, particularly outside of the home. Furthermore, many people enjoy the taste of different types of bottled water, which justifies paying a higher price than for tap water. It is still affordable for many consumers. **6/10 marks awarded.**

(d) g The answer relies heavily on Extract B for explaining the external costs associated with an increase in production and consumption of bottled water. It tends to copy the information in the extract, offering little development, and market failure is not explored (1 knowledge and 1 application mark); furthermore, no reference is made to private costs, such as raw materials, machinery and workers' wages. An external cost diagram is provided but without explanation or application to bottled water (1 knowledge mark). This part of the answer is a Level 2, being a narrow response with limited chains of reasoning. It could be improved by explaining the free market ($0P_e$ and $0Q_e$) and social optimum positions ($0P_1$ and $0Q_1$) and also the triangle of welfare loss (XYW).

including plastic and water companies. Labour productivity at work can also increase from a well hydrated workforce.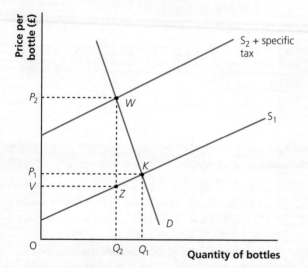

There are also benefits for people's health in consuming bottled water, which helps prevent dehydration and possible illnesses resulting from this. Consequently, once external benefits are included, the social optimum output would be higher and the net welfare loss lower. Private benefits include the utility people gain from consuming bottled water.

(e) Specific taxes and regulations both have their merits in reducing the external costs associated with the production and consumption of bottled water. Specific taxes act to increase production costs which are passed on to consumers via higher prices. In the case of the 5p tax on plastic bags it has been very successful, leading to a dramatic fall in demand. If a similar tax was applied to plastic water bottles, it could also reduce demand as shown in the diagram. Price is increased from P_1 to P_2 and quantity decreased from Q_1 to Q_2. The total tax revenue collected is P_2WZV. This could be used to help clean up the waste from plastic bottles.

Tax on bottled water

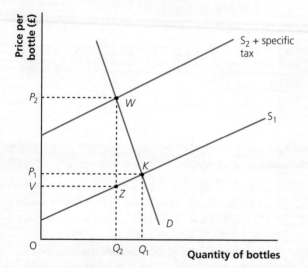

However, many consumers may be more willing to pay the higher price due to convenience and the belief that bottled water is important for health. Consequently, demand is likely to be price inelastic, so having a small impact on reducing overall consumption. Unless the tax is large and hypothecated to be used for cleaning up plastic waste, it is unlikely to internalise the external costs. Furthermore, there is already 20% VAT on bottled water and this has not prevented market growth.

Regulations could be more effective in solving plastic waste from bottled water. For example, legislation could be passed to ensure that all plastic bottles are recyclable or that manufacturers have to offer a money back deposit scheme on their return. 🄳 However, regulations have their own drawbacks in terms of the costs of setting up a manageable deposit scheme — presumably the retailers will be responsible for collecting the bottles returned by customers. 🄼

🄳 In the third paragraph the student refers to regulations using examples provided in Extract B, but does not really develop the benefits of, for example, the threat of prosecution, fines and closure of firms (1 application mark). 🄼 However, the effectiveness of regulations is questioned in the last sentence (1 evaluation mark). Overall, the answer achieves Level 2 for knowledge, application and analysis (6 from 9), which could be better developed through more chains of reasoning.

11/15 marks awarded.

In terms of evaluation, the response reaches Level 3 (5 out of 6); it does not quite compare the relative merits of the two forms of government intervention. For example, taxes offer the consumer choice and operate via the price mechanism, but may be ineffective if demand is price inelastic and the revenue raised is not used to deal with plastic pollution; by contrast, regulations are compulsory, costly to implement and block the operation of the price mechanism, but could be more effective, depending on their enforcement. Another evaluation technique which might be offered here is to suggest that both measures may complement each other if used together.

Total score: 33/50 marks = grade B

Question 2 The UK housing market

Table 1 Comparison of average house prices, annual earnings and population growth for London and northwest England, 2018

Region	Average house price (£)	Average annual earnings, full-time employee (£)	Projected population growth, 2016–26 (%)
London	£486,304	£37,087	8.8
Northwest	£163,487	£27,539	3.4

Source: Office for National Statistics

Extract A Rising house prices amid supply shortages

Average house prices in the UK increased from £171,000 in August 2012 to £233,000 in August 2018, caused by demand-side and supply-side factors. Low mortgage interest rates and the availability of house loans have played an important part. There are also severe shortages of skilled building workers, especially in London, following the uncertainty over the UK's membership of the EU single market. Shortages of building materials such as bricks and cement have also increased, forcing firms to look to imports. Furthermore, planning regulations that protect the countryside around urban areas make it difficult for developers to meet the rising demand for housing.

Extract B Green belt land under attack

The Campaign to Protect Rural England (CPRE) reports that 460,000 homes are planned to be built on land removed from green belt protection. The green belt refers to land surrounding urban areas that is protected from development, which would otherwise lead to sprawling cities and environmental damage. Local councils are allocating green belt land for development to meet central government house-building targets — otherwise they risk losing control over where the new house building takes place. The CPRE said that building new homes should instead be focused on brownfield land (land that has previously been built on and is now derelict). There is enough brownfield land to build more than a million homes.

Extract C Private rental market growing

Rising house prices for owner occupiers over the past decade have led to a fall in home ownership and an increase in the number of people renting from private landlords. Between 2007 and 2017 home ownership fell from 71% to 63% of households whereas private rental rose from 12.7% to 20.3%. With home ownership out of reach and social housing unavailable, millions of people have no option but to rent from a private landlord. A housing survey conducted by the Office for National Statistics found that 46% of 25–34-year-olds now live in private rented property, compared with just 27% in 2007. The beneficiaries of the rental boom are landlords, who have increasingly displaced first-time buyers over the past two decades. There are now 2 million landlords who own 5 million properties in the UK.

Private rents are high — the total amount paid by tenants in the UK soared to more than £51 billion in 2017, more than twice the amount paid in 2007. This sum is rapidly catching up with the £57 billion paid by homeowners who have mortgages. Many tenants pay more than half their salaries in rent and struggle to meet other costs including food bills. Renting property is already unaffordable for many. This has led to calls for the government to impose rent controls to alleviate the housing shortage.

(a) With reference to Table 1, explain two likely reasons for the difference in average house prices between London and the northwest. [5 marks]

> This is the only question in the data response with no evaluation marks. All the marks are for knowledge, application and analysis. Ensure you refer to Table 1 in your answer to gain the application marks: for example, by calculating the average regional house price to earnings ratios. The data also provide likely reasons why regional house price differences exist — differences in earnings and population growth.

(b) With reference to Table 1 and your own knowledge, examine how differences in average regional house prices might affect the geographical mobility of labour. [8 marks]

> It is a good idea to define the key term in the question — namely, the geographical mobility of labour — to gain 1 knowledge mark. Make sure the data are explicitly used in order to gain application and analysis marks: for example, London average earnings are 35% above those of the northwest, yet average house prices are 197% higher. This suggests it will be extremely difficult for workers to move to London to take available jobs due to much higher housing costs. There are also 2 marks available for an evaluative comment here, so make sure one is offered. Use of the data will count towards the quantitative aspects of the assessment.

(c) With reference to Extracts A and B, discuss whether the supply of new-build housing is likely to be price elastic or price inelastic.

[12 marks]

> Ensure both extracts are referred to in your answer and that key determinants of price elasticity of supply are linked to the information provided. Although it is possible to gain the full 4 evaluation marks from developing one point, it is wise to offer two comments here.

(d) With reference to Extract C, assess the likely impact of rising house prices (for owner occupiers) on the private rental market. Use a supply and demand diagram in your answer.

[10 marks]

> Consider both consumers (tenants) and producers (landlords) in the private rental market. Also be prepared to use economic concepts underlying the question: for example, cross elasticity of demand. Make sure your answer focuses on the question set, namely the impact for the private rental market — it is easy to stray into other markets here.

(e) To what extent might the introduction of rent controls on private rental housing alleviate the housing shortage? Use a suitable demand and supply diagram in your answer.

[15 marks]

> The command phrase 'To what extent' invites you to consider the degree to which you agree with the statement, supporting your argument with evidence. Be prepared to challenge the statement — you might not agree with it. It is useful to consider both sides of the argument to secure up to 6 evaluation marks. Ensure that a diagram is offered or your marks will be capped, usually to a Level 2 response (a maximum of 6 out of 9 knowledge, application and analysis marks).

Student answer

(a) Average house prices in London (£486,304) are almost three times more expensive than average house prices in the northwest (£163,487). a The first reason is due to average earnings being higher in London (£37,087) than in the northwest (£27,539). This means people in London are able to borrow more in order to purchase property, leading to higher demand and house prices. People who earn more can afford to take out larger house loans (mortgages) in order to buy property. b A second likely reason is the projected increase in the population in London of 8.8% between 2016 and 2026, which is higher than that for the northwest (3.4%), again leading to greater demand and price pressures. c

(b) The difference in average regional house prices is likely to reduce geographical mobility of labour. It will make it harder for workers in the northwest to take available jobs in London since they may be unable to afford to purchase housing. d Buying a house is often the single most expensive financial

(a) a The student recognises that house prices are almost three times more expensive in London compared to the northwest (1 knowledge mark). b The first reason makes use of the average regional earnings data and is then linked to the affordability of taking out house loans (1 application and 1 analysis mark). c The second reason refers to regional population growth rates and is then linked to the relative demand for housing (1 application and 1 analysis mark).
5/5 marks awarded.

(b) d The student understands the meaning of geographical mobility of labour and indicates that it would be reduced by significant differences in regional house prices (1 + 1 knowledge marks).

commitment people make in their lifetime and it takes up a significant proportion of disposable income. London house prices are clearly unaffordable for all but the highest income earners in society. **e** Table 1 shows that although the average London worker earns around 35% more than the average worker in the northwest, this difference is much smaller than the average house price difference (almost 300% more expensive in London). Consequently, even though a worker moving to London can expect to earn more, it is still too low to be able to afford to buy a property. **f**

However, regional house price differences make it easier for workers in London to take available jobs in the northwest and other regions where housing is much cheaper. So the geographical mobility of labour could be enhanced if more jobs are created outside of London where workers could relocate to. **g**

(c) Price elasticity of supply refers to the responsiveness of supply to changes in the price of a good. Information in the extract indicates that the supply of new housing is likely to be price inelastic (where the proportional rise in supply is less than the proportional rise in price). **h**

There appear to be three major constraints on supply: first, Extract A refers to a shortage of skilled building workers such as bricklayers and plumbers, which has been made worse by concerns over Brexit. There is uncertainty over whether labour from the EU will be allowed to continue to work in the UK. It has also deterred many would-be EU migrants coming to the UK to work. It means property developers have to offer higher wages and wait for more people to be trained before responding to the increase in house prices; second, there is a shortage of building materials which further delays the ability of developers to respond to rising house prices. It increases the average time taken to build housing; third, the tight planning regulations on building new housing, especially in urban areas. It takes a long time for developers to gain approval for building new homes and often there are objections by local residents who want to maintain access to open spaces. **i**

To evaluate, it is not surprising that supply is inelastic given a 36% increase in house prices between 2012 and 2018. It would be extremely difficult for new-builds to keep up with such a rapid price increase, particularly given the nature of construction, which requires many different types of skilled labour to be co-ordinated to do specific jobs at certain times in the building process. **j** However, Extract B refers to the government relaxing planning regulations on green belt land to speed up

e The lifetime financial commitment involved in buying a house is mentioned and then linked to the unaffordability of property in London (1 application and 1 analysis mark). **f** The reason why housing in London is typically unaffordable to most people is explained by making effective use of the data in Table 1. This shows the much larger differential between regional average house prices and regional average earnings in London compared to the northwest. Consequently, most households do not earn enough to be able to purchase property in London (1 application and 1 analysis mark). A top Level 3 mark is achieved here. **g** The final paragraph offers an interesting evaluative comment, suggesting that geographical mobility of labour might be improved for people relocating from London to other regions, since property prices are so much cheaper elsewhere (2 evaluation marks). **8/8 marks awarded.**

(c) **h** The student understands price elasticity of supply and applies the concept to new-build housing (1 knowledge and 1 application mark). **i** Three reasons are identified from the extracts and then well developed to explain why supply is likely to be price inelastic (1 knowledge and 1 application mark; 2 + 2 analysis marks). A top Level 3 mark is achieved here. **j** Two evaluation comments are offered: the first makes use of data in Extract A to discuss the magnitude of house price increases and the difficulty of supply responding to such increases;

housing developments. According to the CPRE, enough green belt land has been released from protection to build an extra 460,000 homes over the next few years. This means in the long run, supply of new housing may become less price inelastic (more elastic).

(d) Owner-occupied and private rental housing are substitutes and so have a positive cross elasticity of demand. Extract C mentions that an increase in the price of owner-occupied housing has caused an increase in demand for private rental housing. The diagram shows an increase in demand from D_1 to D_2 pushing up rents from R_1 to R_2 and quantity from Q_1 to Q_2. ⬚ With regards to landlords, total revenue and income have increased as they are able to raise rents and exploit their advantage in the market.

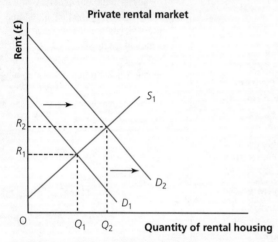

Private rental market

Extract C states that total private rental payments were £51 billion in 2017 — almost as high as the amount paid by owner occupiers with their mortgages. The number of private landlords has also increased to 2 million, having 5 million rental properties between them. ⬚ By contrast, many tenants are struggling to pay their rent and risk falling behind with payments and even being evicted. Also some tenants spend so much on rent that they struggle to pay other bills, such as food and transport. ⬚

To evaluate, it is unrealistic to assume that the private rental market will continue on its upward trend. Ceteris paribus does not hold in the real world; the high rents appear unsustainable and demand is likely to dry up as many potential renters are forced to remain at home with their parents. Furthermore, there could be a recession which reduces demand for private renting, or a major government building programme for social housing, increasing the supply of a close substitute. ⬚

(e) Rent controls are a form of maximum pricing. This is where a maximum monthly rent or price ceiling is set for a rental property, usually backed by government legislation. Such a measure appears to have unintended consequences and it is unlikely to alleviate the housing shortage since there is less incentive for private landlords to rent out their properties at lower prices. It also means that demand for rental properties will rise due to the lower charge, leading to excess demand. 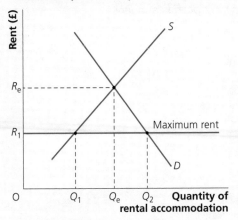 This is shown by the diagram where the government sets a maximum rent of OR_1 which is below the free market rent of OR_e. Supply contracts to OQ_1 and demand extends to OQ_2 leading to a shortage of private rental property of Q_1Q_2. It seems that government intervention distorts the operation of the price mechanism and leads to an inefficient allocation of resources, especially in the long run if the rent controls remain. ⓖ

Maximum price in the private rental market

There are also problems for the government in monitoring and enforcing maximum rent controls. Extract C refers to 5 million private rental properties which will take a lot of inspectors a long time to check the rents. There is a danger of a hidden market or shadow market being created, where some tenants pay more than the maximum rent to ensure they obtain a desirable property to live. Such illegal markets place tenants at risk from exploitation. ⓣ

However, in evaluation of rent controls, some economists believe they can help alleviate the housing shortage. They can reduce exploitation of tenants and ensure that rents are set at affordable levels. It also means that people on relatively low incomes might be able to afford to rent property. Also if the supply of rental property is price inelastic, there might only be a small reduction in rental properties on the market. ⓢ Landlords may have little alternative and so accept a lower return from their properties. It could also be argued that rent controls will reduce the incentive for buy-to-let investors and so make it easier for others to get on the property ladder as these properties become available to buy. ⓣ

(e) ⓟ An explanation of maximum rent controls is given along with an answer to the question — that they are unlikely to reduce the housing shortage. This is a good way to begin your answer for higher mark base questions (1 knowledge, 1 application and 1 analysis mark). ⓖ Relevant diagrammatic analysis and an explanation of how rent controls could worsen the housing shortage is then offered (1 knowledge, 1 application and 1 analysis mark). ⓣ The possibility of illegal hidden rental markets is also addressed, reinforcing the student's view that rent controls do not work (1 knowledge, 1 application and 1 analysis mark). A top Level 3 answer has been achieved. ⓢ and ⓣ Two evaluation comments are made which suggest that rent controls could have a plausible role in reducing the housing shortage (3 + 3 evaluation marks). Clearly this a superior answer.
15/15 marks awarded.

Total score: 50/50 marks = top grade A

Section C

Extended open-response questions

The final part of the exam paper, section C, involves selecting one extended open-response question from a choice of two offering up to 25 marks. Question 1 below considers government subsidies to public transport and Question 2 is on minimum pricing of alcohol.

As mentioned earlier, there is a 'levels'-based approach to marking these questions. There is a total of 16 knowledge, application and analysis marks and 9 evaluation marks available from the 25-mark question.

Question 1 Government subsidies to public transport

The UK has one of the most congested road systems of all developed countries in the world, costing motorists over £30 billion a year.

Evaluate the case for increasing government subsidies to public transport as a means of reducing road traffic congestion.

[25 marks]

The opening statement provides information on how serious road traffic congestion has become and it is useful to include the numerical cost in your answer. The command word 'evaluate' invites you to consider the effectiveness of public transport subsidies in reducing road congestion. You should focus on how subsidies are meant to influence the market and be prepared to include diagrammatic analysis. Follow this up with reasons why it might be effective (such as lower fares and improved service) and then its limitations; these might include the problem of public transport being a weak substitute for private motor vehicle transport.

Note: Efforts to break down the marks into individual components for extended open-response essay questions is rather contrived, especially as examiners will consider the overall quality of the answer and then match it to the appropriate level in the mark scheme. Examiners will expect relevant definitions, well-explained diagrams, economic analysis and application to the question. They will also expect two or more evaluative comments. All this should be undertaken in the structure of a mini-essay, with an introduction, main body and conclusion.

Student answer

Public transport subsidies are government grants aimed at increasing the supply and lowering the price of rail and bus travel. Their purpose is to encourage motorists to leave their cars at home and use bus and rail transport instead, helping to reduce road traffic congestion. a Private motor vehicles and public transport are substitutes with a positive cross elasticity of demand. This means that government subsidies, which lower the price of public transport, will cause a decrease in demand for private motor vehicles as motorists switch to using buses and trains. The closer the substitutes, the greater the impact of public transport subsidies in reducing road congestion. b

a The introduction is clear and simple, explaining the meaning and purpose of subsidies (2 knowledge marks). b The relationship between public transport and private motoring is explained via the use of cross elasticity of demand (1 knowledge, 1 application and 1 analysis mark).

Subsidies provided to bus and rail firms act to reduce their production costs and so shift supply outwards, helping to lower market price. This is shown in the diagram where the unit subsidy increases supply from S_1 to S_2, leading to a fall in equilibrium price from P_1 to P_2 and a consequent rise in number of passengers from Q_1 to Q_2. The total subsidy spending is shown by the area $GLFP_2$, with P_1TFP_2 being transferred to consumers via lower prices. The remaining subsidy area P_1GLT is gained by producers. c

c This section offers relevant and accurate diagrammatic analysis of how public transport subsidies help reduce road congestion (1 knowledge, 2 application and 4 analysis marks).

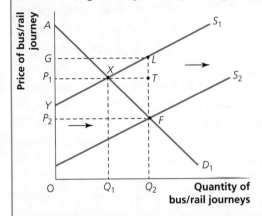

Large towns and cities are often where the greatest road congestion tends to occur, which makes it important to direct the extra government subsidies to these areas. Some funds could be allocated to improve the quality of buses and trains, for example, more comfortable seats and more reliable services. Some funds could also be spent on increasing market knowledge through apps on live services so that people become aware of how long they have to wait before the next bus or train arrives. This could reduce information gaps between consumers and producers. Used in these ways, public transport subsidies should help reduce the £30 billion road congestion bill. d

However, there are limitations to the effectiveness of increasing public transport subsidies, for example, many private motorists prefer the convenience and safety of using their cars to get from one place to another for things like work and shopping. This suggests public transport is a weak substitute for private motor vehicles. e

Furthermore, demand for public transport may be price inelastic which suggests government subsidies will not increase the number of passengers by much, as motorists still prefer to use their cars. If this is the case, traffic congestion will remain. It also implies that the extra buses and trains put into service will operate with a lot of empty seats and so do not give taxpayers value for money. Perhaps the extra public transport subsidies could be better spent elsewhere to reduce road congestion, for example, by targeting improvements to problem locations. This may involve road widening schemes, repairing potholes and inserting traffic lights to increase traffic flow. f

d Further development is offered, explaining how public transport subsidies could be spent (1 application and 3 analysis marks). *This part of the essay achieves Level 4 (16 out of 16 marks), where economic ideas are carefully selected and applied appropriately, demonstrating logical chains of reasoning.* e *and* f *These two paragraphs contain evaluative comments which consider why many motorists prefer using private cars and also whether the demand for public transport is price inelastic, reducing the effectiveness of government subsidies (2 + 5 evaluation marks).*

To conclude, increasing public transport subsidies can help reduce road congestion, but on their own, they are likely to be ineffective. There needs to be a combination of measures used together, for example, the introduction of road congestion charges in all major towns and cities, higher motor vehicle taxes and promotion of more car sharing schemes. Otherwise public transport subsidies may prove to be a waste of taxpayers' money and lead to government failure. g

g The conclusion offers a judgement on how public transport subsidies might be part of a range of measures required to reduce road traffic congestion (2 evaluation marks). It is a good idea to offer an overall judgement in the conclusion, which can be quite thought provoking. *This part of the essay achieves Level 3 (9 out of 9 marks), where the evaluation recognises different viewpoints and is critical of the assumptions made, enabling informed judgements.*
25/25 marks = top grade A.

Question 2 Minimum price on alcohol

In May 2018, the Scottish government introduced a minimum price of 50p per unit of alcohol.

Evaluate whether a minimum price is the most effective way to reduce market failure associated with the overconsumption of alcohol. Use an appropriate supply and demand diagram in your answer.

[25 marks]

The opening statement provides a context for the minimum price scheme and it is useful to include this in your answer. Also make sure a supply and demand diagram depicting the minimum price is included with an explanation or risk being capped (usually at Level 3, a maximum of 12 from 16 knowledge, application and analysis marks). Although the focus of the answer should be minimum pricing, the question is worded in such a way as to invite consideration of other suitable measures which could correct market failure: for example, regulations and indirect taxation. A paragraph investigating these alternative measures is recommended.

Student answer

The overconsumption of alcohol is regarded as a major cause of health problems such as liver disease and so can lead to a reduction in the quality of life and life expectancy for heavy drinkers. The alcohol market is typically associated with market failure, where the operation of the price mechanism leads to an inefficient allocation of resources and a net welfare loss. This is due to the existence of information gaps and external costs that lead to some consumers drinking far more than is good for themselves and for society as a whole. a

A minimum price represents a legal price floor at which alcohol can be sold. It is a type of 'nudge' measure which uses the price mechanism to influence consumer behaviour, whilst at the same time maintaining consumer choice. A minimum price on alcohol would have to be set above the free market price in order to have an effect. This is shown in the diagram where the minimum price of P_2 causes a contraction in demand from Q_e to Q_1. There is an income effect on the market as alcohol becomes less

a The introduction explains why the overconsumption of alcohol is a problem (2 application marks) and goes on to define market failure and the types relevant here, namely external costs and information gaps (2 knowledge marks).

affordable, especially for people on low incomes. There is also a substitution effect as consumers may look to cheaper alternatives such as soft drinks.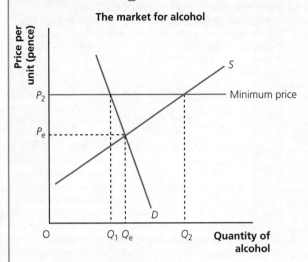

The market for alcohol

Furthermore, the minimum price is unlikely to raise supply as firms quickly realise they cannot sell so much due to it being more expensive and so the excess supply of alcohol of Q_1Q_2 is likely to be temporary. It might also encourage these firms to switch production to non-alcoholic drinks. c

However, there are limitations to minimum prices that could reduce its effectiveness in correcting market failure. Alcohol tends to be habit forming and even addictive and so demand is likely to be price inelastic. It means that consumers are still likely to buy alcohol despite the price rise. Ironically, alcohol firms might even gain additional revenue. d Furthermore, the minimum price set may be too low to have much impact on deterring consumption. In Scotland it was just 50p for a glass of wine or beer which is hardly likely to discourage people from drinking, even those on low incomes. e

b Relevant diagrammatic analysis is provided on how a minimum price can reduce consumption of alcohol, including both the income and substitution effects (4 analysis and 2 application marks). c The responsiveness of drinks firms to the minimum price is also considered, linking back to the diagram (2 analysis marks). No consideration of additional measures to correct excess alcohol consumption is offered: for example, regulations and indirect taxation. *This part of the essay achieves Level 3 (12 out of a total of 16 marks), where economic analysis is clear and coherent, with chains of reasoning, but lacks balance.* d and e The evaluation part of the essay questions the effectiveness of minimum pricing since demand for alcohol tends to be price inelastic and the size of thc price control is also quite small (3 + 2 evaluation marks). Evaluation could better target the types of market failure such as information gaps and external costs. For example, minimum pricing does not deal with information gaps — where some people drink more than the maximum health guidelines per week through ignorance. This requires public health campaigns and regulations which compel firms to state the units of alcohol being consumed on each drink. Furthermore, minimum pricing does little to internalise the external costs of consuming too much alcohol, such as increased pressure on healthcare services and lost productivity due to absenteeism from work. Instead, alternative measures are likely to be more effective, such as hypothecated indirect taxes. *This part of the essay achieves Level 2 (5 out of a total of 9 marks), where evaluation includes developed chains of reasoning but is unbalanced.* **Total score: 17/25 marks = grade B.**

Knowledge check answers

1 The opportunity cost of you staying on at school to take A-levels is the next best alternative: for example, earning income from a job or joining an apprenticeship scheme to learn a trade.

2 Opportunity cost can be shown by a movement along a production possibility frontier: for example, from position A to B. An extra 10 units of manufactured goods are obtained at the expense of 5 units of services.

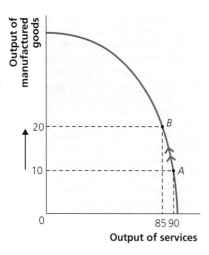

3 There must be unemployed resources in the economy — spare capacity exists.

4 An outward shift of the production possibility frontier might be caused by an increase in the quality or quantity of labour, an increase in capital goods (investment), new technology, enterprise and discovery of natural resources.

5 The division of labour means workers become more skilled at what they do through experience and repetition of tasks. It thereby leads to greater output.

6 The UK is a mixed economy, since both private enterprise and the government decide how resources are allocated for production and distribution.

7 As the price of a good falls, it becomes more affordable for consumers to buy with their income. Also, it becomes relatively cheaper than substitute goods and so some consumers will switch to buying it.

8 A change in the price of the good in question. A rise in price will lead to a contraction in demand and a fall in price will lead to an extension in demand.

9 The main factors include a change in price of substitute or complementary goods and a change in income or tastes. Note that changes in the price of the good will not shift the demand curve.

10 The minus sign means there is an inverse relationship between the change in price and the change in demand. Thus, a rise in price will cause a fall in quantity demanded. The demand curve has a negative gradient.

11 The answer indicates how much a 1% change in price causes demand to change by. For example, an answer of 3 means that a 1% change in price will lead to a 3% change in demand for the good.

12 If a firm knows the price elasticity of demand for the good it produces then it may be able to increase total revenue by changing the price. If demand is inelastic, a rise in price will increase total revenue; if demand is elastic, a fall in price will increase total revenue.

13 If the government knows the price elasticity of demand for a particular good then it will have an idea of the impact that an indirect tax will have on it. For example, a tax placed on a good with inelastic demand should lead to a high tax yield and have relatively little impact on demand.

14 Normal goods have a positive income elasticity of demand; as real income rises, demand for the good also rises. Inferior goods have a negative income elasticity of demand; as real income rises, demand for the good falls.

15 Complementary goods have a negative cross elasticity of demand: for example, a fall in price of computer games consoles will cause an increase in demand for computer games software. Substitute goods have a positive cross elasticity of demand: for example, a rise in price of beef may cause an increase in demand for lamb.

16 As the price of a good rises, there is an incentive to supply more since the firm might achieve higher profits. It is also able to cover the extra costs involved in producing more of the good.

17 A change in the price of the good in question. A rise in price will lead to an extension in supply and a fall in price will lead to a contraction in supply.

18 The main factors include a change in costs of production, technology, the ability of firms to enter and exit an industry, indirect taxes and government subsidies. Note that changes in the price of the good will not shift the supply curve.

19 A positive number means there is a direct relationship between the change in price and the change in quantity supplied. Thus, a rise in price will cause a rise in the quantity supplied. The supply curve has a positive gradient.

20 The figure indicates by how much a 1% change in price causes quantity supplied to change. For example, an answer of 2 means that a 1% change in price will lead to a 2% change in quantity supplied of the good.

21 For most goods, supply tends to be relatively price inelastic in the short run as some factor inputs are fixed in quantity, but becomes relatively price elastic in the long run when all factor inputs are variable.

22 If supply exceeds demand, price will fall, leading to an extension in demand and a contraction in supply. Eventually, equilibrium position is reached.

23 If demand exceeds supply, the price will rise, leading to an extension in supply and contraction in demand. Eventually, equilibrium position is reached.

24 A decrease in demand for a good will cause its price to fall and so lead to a decrease in producer surplus and consumer surplus.

25 A decrease in supply of a good will cause its price to rise but a fall in both the consumer surplus and producer surplus.

26 A specific tax is placed as a fixed amount per unit of good and causes an inward parallel shift in the supply curve. An *ad valorem* tax is placed as a percentage of the price of a good and causes an inward pivotal shift in the supply curve.

27 A unit subsidy will shift the supply curve outwards (an increase in supply) and reduce the equilibrium price.

28 Alternative views of consumer behaviour are those which assume consumers do not always aim or behave in a way that maximises total utility from their expenditure.

29 Consumers may not maximise total utility due to: copying other consumers rather than thinking for themselves; keeping with their habits rather than making changes; difficulties in computation.

30 Social costs are the total of private costs and external costs.

31 Social benefits are the total of private benefits and external benefits.

32 Market equilibrium is the output position where marginal private benefits (*MPB*) equal marginal private costs (*MPC*). Externalities are ignored. However, the social optimum is where marginal social benefits (*MSB*) equal marginal social costs (*MSC*).

33 The welfare loss triangle is the area on an externality diagram that depicts the excess of social costs over social benefits for a given level of output.

34 The welfare gain triangle is the area on an externality diagram that depicts the excess of social benefits over social costs for a given output level.

35 External costs cause market failure since they are ignored by the price mechanism and lead to a welfare loss. For example, a person smoking leads to passive smoking for others, who suffer but are not compensated.

36 External benefits cause market failure since they are ignored by the price mechanism and lead to a loss of potential welfare. For example, a person paying for a vaccination will reduce the risk of disease for others but this benefit is not accounted for by the price mechanism and so under-provision occurs.

37 On a hot day a public beach might become so overcrowded that people compete for space on the beach — there may be rivalry in consumption. A public beach might also be sold off to a property developer who restricts access to members of the public.

38 The free-rider problem is where an individual is able to consume a good without paying for it. Consequently, there is no incentive for firms to supply the good in a free market.

39 Public goods are a type of market failure since there would be no provision or very little provision of them in a free market. This is due to the free-rider problem — where it is possible to consume the goods without paying for them. Consequently, there is no profit incentive for firms to provide them.

40 Imperfect market information leads to market failure because consumers and producers may make decisions on buying or selling a good which reduce their overall welfare.

41 The key reason for government intervention is to correct market failure so that markets work more efficiently and there is less welfare loss.

42 High taxes are placed on tobacco, alcohol and petrol in order to internalise external costs. They are a way of making the polluters pay for these costs. In addition, they provide significant tax revenue to the government, since demand is typically price inelastic for these goods.

43 The government typically subsidises goods which have significant external benefits in production or consumption: for example, renewable energy sources, public transport and healthcare.

44 A maximum price in the house rental sector will help low-income families afford to rent property and reduce the danger of exploitation.

45 Maximum price controls may reduce both the supply and quality of rental housing, leading to a greater shortage in the market.

46 A minimum price for alcohol and sugar will reduce the costs associated with these products: for example, crime, alcoholism, obesity, pressure on the healthcare service and absenteeism from work.

47 Disadvantages include the danger of shadow markets being formed as well as increasing the price of goods for low-income households.

48 A 'cap and trade' scheme is where the government limits the amount of pollution that firms are able to emit but also allows them to buy and sell pollution permits between themselves.

49 A system of tradable pollution permits was introduced in order to limit pollution emissions from heavy industry. The EU believes that by creating a market for pollution it can help reduce overall carbon emissions.

50 If too many pollution permits are issued then the price falls so much that there is little incentive for firms to cut back on emissions; if too few permits are issued then the price of permits rises so much as to make EU industry uncompetitive in global markets.

Index

Note: **bold** page numbers refer to definitions.

Index